Advance Praise from the Writing Community for
Confessions of a Christian Mystic

"Raw-boned. Unflinching. Gut-level honest. This is the kind of real that explodes! River Jordan bears her soul as she recounts her lifelong search for God and meaning. Read it and be prepared for the barn doors on your own beliefs to be blown wide open."
—Bren McClain, author of *One Good Mama Bone*

"In her latest book, River Jordan confesses to having a pathological hunger for God. To guide those who would seek Him, she says the world must have its mystics—its Joans and its Johns. And, I would add, its Rivers. Jordan raises the bar that writers like Anne Lamott have set, as she shows us how to find the mystical divine—which she calls 'God's wild card'—in the messy stuff of everyday life. This is a must-read for everyone who loves the beauty of language and the power of story. Both can lead us to communion with God when those words are in the gifted hands of River Jordan."
—Susan Cushman, author of *Cherry Bomb* and *Tangles and Plaques: A Mother and Daughter Face Alzheimer's*, and editor of *A Second Blooming: Becoming the Women We Are Meant to Be* and *Southern Writers on Writing*

"River Jordan once again explores the spiritual aspect of the human journey through her tender lens. She nudges us out of our comfort zones and into realms of personal discovery. With a master's hand, she peels open every raw corner of her own experiences so that we close the book forever shaped by this soul-stirring story. Delivered in small but powerful doses,

River's words offer good medicine to any heart that has known hunger or hurt, love or loss. This is a book for any heart that dares to remain open in this great, big, beautiful, cruel world."
—Julie Cantrell, *New York Times* and *USA TODAY* bestselling author of *Perennials*

"If you're burned out on the quick-fix schemes and robot-speak of today's Christian literature, get in the truck and take a mystical road trip with River Jordan. (Don't worry, 'mystic' just means searching for Something Bigger, and River is honest enough to admit she hasn't figured it out yet.)

"Raw and real as a gravel road through rural Alabama, River's *Confessions* is guaranteed to stir your soul and lead you down the wandering path home.

"Here's a book for all us hard-luck, outlaw, C-minus Christians hoping, wandering, and trying to hold on. It's the antidote, if you will, to all that church-y syrup and motivational BS packaged as 'inspirational' when it only makes us feel even more messed up than we did before. Stripped down and honest to the bone, River Jordan's *Confessions of a Christian Mystic* will not only bring you closer to Jesus—that misfit friend of sinners—it just might help you find yourself."
—J. M. Blaine, author of *Midnight, Jesus & Me*

"In *Confessions of a Christian Mystic*, River Jordan's adventures in faith are both honest and revelatory. We are extraordinarily fortunate to travel alongside River Jordan as she speaks to us with wit, wisdom, and clarity about the path she has taken, the mystical understandings she has discovered, and wounds revealed and healed. In chapters that connect us with everything from our faith to our doubt, this is a book for everyone forging ahead on their own mystical journey. With her storytelling magic, Jordan brings us into her world while asking the impor-

tant questions about faith, purpose, and love. A profound book to keep on your shelf, and to give to those you love."
—Patti Callahan Henry, *New York Times* bestselling author

"In *Confessions of a Christian Mystic*, writer and novelist River Jordan shares her lifelong spiritual journey to find her place in this world and to understand the nature of the next. This book is an honest look at the messy nature of belief, and Jordan reminds us all that glimpses of the divine are there for us to see if we have the wisdom and the strength to peel back the layers of doubt. The series of essays in this collection range from the wonderings of an innocent child about whether God lives in the clouds to the heartfelt worries of a mother with grown children wandering in harm's way. In each, the author's spiritual glass is more than full enough to quench the thirst that comes from wanting to know. *Confessions of a Christian Mystic* is a book for our times, and one that you should read with an open mind and a full heart."
—Raymond L. Atkins, author of *Set List*, *South of the Etowah*, and *Sweetwater Blues*

"From growing up surrounded by a band of strong, faith-filled Southern women to encountering God while sleeping in an Airstream trailer, *Confessions of a Christian Mystic* allowed me to glimpse behind acclaimed author River Jordan's veil, proving my supposition that she has led—and continues to lead—an extraordinary life. Part American history, part autobiography, while filled with River Jordan's penchant for lyrical writing, *Confessions of a Christian Mystic* is an intimate glimpse at one woman's spiritual journey that encourages us to look at our own journeys with the same introspection and gratitude."
—Jolina Petersheim, bestselling author of *How the Light Gets In*

"What I love about *Confessions* is that it reads like a conversation with a best friend about all the big questions. A conversation where there is room for me, too. A conversation with the pieces of the puzzle we experience and then try in vain to assemble into the whole truth...and in doing so sometimes assemble OUR whole truth. At least for this moment. Because the finer points of our truth can be dynamic."

—Kaya McLaren, author of *How I Came to Sparkle Again* and *On the Divinity of Second Chances*

Advance Praise from the Reading Community for
Confessions of a Christian Mystic

"I am a puddle. *Confessions of a Christian Mystic* brought me to tears with River Jordan's unsettling honesty and transparency. At this same instant, though, I want to scream for joy and to run up and down the hallways, shove copies of *Confessions* into everyone's hand, and insist they sit down *right now* and read every word. They've got to. For their own sanity, for their salvation, and for their survival.

"This collection is more than a masterful piece of creation. It is, as sincerely and honestly as I can express, a life changer.

"To borrow River's words, it is 'hauntingly clinging.' I don't think I'll ever shake my personal *ah-ha*s and the *me-too*s as I moved from chapter to chapter to chapter. River's willingness and fearlessness to be so vulnerable and exposed have validated my soul's experiences. I, too, have seen the gold fill the room and have known the Spirit was there and moving. I have been consumed by the literal light and been changed by my own take-my-breath-away encounters with God and His inexplicable time- and place-shifting powers— but dared to only share what I had seen and felt with just a very, very few (and almost all of them looked back at me as if I was losing it). River has looked at the same things viewed by everyone else on the planet but has seen some things entirely differently. She also has been brave enough to tell this same world what they have not seen. But should. And could.

"I don't know what to say or how to say it, except…She

gets it. And she's put it out there. I can't wait for the rest of the world to get it, too."

—Lea Anne Brandon, director of communications, MS Department of Child Protection Services

"River's ability and willingness to probe into the deepest part of herself is what has always characterized her work, and *Confessions of a Christian Mystic* is no exception. In fact, it is the epitome of her collective work, always a glimpse of her very human soul. She reminds me to live in the now and not to be distressed in the ordinary life that demands so much of my attention. I'm assured that prayer is often a state of being rather than hidden in the closet, and that both are equally accepted and needed. River shows her map, torn and dirty, with footprints in no particular order, and yet they always lead back to the very heart of our existence. This richness, rawness, heart light, heartbreak, a glimpse beyond the veil, speaks and speaks and speaks."

—Karen Schwettman, FoxTale Book Shoppe, Woodstock, GA

"In River Jordan's *Confessions of a Christian Mystic*, I find good company. And as she says herself, the company we keep matters. The conversations and influences within that fellowship fuel our lives. I find wonderfully good company among storytellers, poets and mystics, dreamers, too. They provide for me a sense of connection to the deeper meaning of things and walk me closer to that place we all yearn for—where love is unconditional and we feel understood—which nurtures fortitude to understand and love in return.

"River's confessions are a gutsy baring of her soul, a stripping down to essentials of what makes us human and seekers after the God Who birthed us and desires us to be in relationship with Him. She writes of fire, ruins, forgiveness, and hope; of love that transcends death and the light that breaks through the cracks in everything. In her personal mystical search, River has uncovered a wealth of nourishment and more. She leads us to the well that waters all our spirits and to an everyday discovery that the Eternal Mystery lives right here under our noses."

—Mary Louise Tucker, Orcas Island, WA

"*Confessions of a Christian Mystic* is a flawless mix of personal memoir, musings on faith, and love letters to the messiness of humanity. I fell head over heels for River's melodious prose and loved basking in her reflections. I can't wait to put this on the shelf with the likes of Anne Lamott, Elizabeth Gilbert, and Nadia Bolz-Weber."

—Catherine Bock, Parnassus Books
inventory manager and adult buyer

Confessions
of a
Christian Mystic

by River Jordan

New York Nashville

FaithWords
Hachette Book Group
1290 Avenue of the Americas, New York, NY 10104
faithwords.com
twitter.com/faithwords

First Edition: April 2019

FaithWords is a division of Hachette Book Group, Inc. The FaithWords name and logo are trademarks of Hachette Book Group, Inc.

The publisher is not responsible for websites (or their content) that are not owned by the publisher.

The Hachette Speakers Bureau provides a wide range of authors for speaking events. To find out more, go to www.hachettespeakersbureau.com or call (866) 376-6591.

"Good Girls Don't Get Naked," "Sometimes Good Girls Get Naked," "Running Naked Is Good for You," "Naked Is Natural," and "Naked Came I" were previously published in the anthology *Southern Sin: True Stories of the Sultry South and Women Behaving Badly,* edited by Lee Gutkind and Beth Ann Fennelly (2014).

Library of Congress Cataloging-in-Publication Data has been applied for.

ISBNs: 978-1-5460-3568-8 (hardcover), 978-1-4555-5364-8 (ebook)

Printed in the United States of America

LSC-C

10 9 8 7 6 5 4 3 2 1

Abyssus abyssum invocat.
(Deep calls to deep.)

Which child is my favorite? Well, that's easy
to tell. The one what's sick till he is well, the
one farthest off till he is home.
>   —Grandmother Estelle,
>   keeper of the family Bible

Contents

Dear Reader

My sons came home from the war. That's where all good stories should begin. My loves came home again. My priceless treasure, found safe and whole. We are once again together in this sacred life. I sit at my desk this morning, that favorite photo of those sons before me. Thinking this alone should fill me up forever with a gratefulness that knows no end. The prayer that ends all prayers: if you do nothing else but this, deliver my child. What mother among us with empty arms would not take on my every burden to hold her child? But in the midst of blessing, even then, there is sometimes that place where the sky comes to an end.

Next to the photo stands a little statue with arms out-stretched. A gift from a friend writing to me that her name was Courage. "You'll always have it now in the middle of everything. No matter what."

People thought I had courage when those sons were both de-ployed, but I did not. I had a strange sustenance that carried me on. Some would call it faith, but I assure you, my faith for the future of all things I hoped for faltered. It was the faith of others that carried me in those days.

I went through a phase where I played Leonard Cohen's

"Hallelujah" over and over and over yet again. I've been broken, and in all the unspoken places. Still, I crawl back to God. I pray he helps me embrace this life completely and be willing to leave it all behind in the same beating of my heart. I think in the end that's what it comes down to. Passionately breaking open at every moment. Clinging to each other every second of each embrace. Being just as hungry to let it all go to stand in that Holy Presence some of us cannot deny.

A divorce this past year from a twenty-year marriage has wiped me clean. I have stared at the page with apprehension—reading the words written a year ago, they seemed foreign. They were funny, yes, in part, but they were missing the gravitas of my current situation. It was as if they had been written from a distant past. I had crossed a deep chasm, not just a year. What goes unseen in heartbreak is a lot.

It's a funny thing, this obstacle at the page. When I am distracted, busy with my grocery lists, my errand runs, here they come. A wild stampede of words, stomping, snorting, demanding, and beautiful. I find my way to the page as soon as time permits and am greeted with my familiar state of staring at the screen. Silence engulfs me. It's as if my muse has been hijacked, held in a frozen, wordless world. I come up empty and full of dread, cold ash dripping from my tongue where fires once leapt. Until I finally realize that it wasn't my words I'd lost; I'd lost a life. I wouldn't write down the words because the story had changed.

Loss is a part of the human experience, and when it finds us we move from one day into the next as if swimming through shadows. In this I am not alone but one of millions who have loved and lost. Like them, I've gone on traveling the road, continuing the journey, weathering the storms that have wrecked me. I am a survivor clinging to a ravaged world I cannot leave, because it is not a place. It is the new landscape of my soul riddled with the devastation of hope and silent dreams.

Seasons change, and we change with them. We die from one life only to rise into another. To walk step by slow and steady step, thankfully, into the new day. To experience the miracle that is resurrection.

I have a pathological hunger for God. One I have preferred to sweep behind the curtain that is my sense of humor. To tell stories of my messy moments. To concentrate on my sloppy humanity.

You hold in hand my confessions. They came at the price of revealing what I believe. With the added cost of being vulnerable, exposed. A revelation that pulls back the skin of me. I am raw and open for you to see. Here are the bones of my mistakes, the overworked muscles of my mind. Here's my soulful longing for the divine. These words are my blood to the page. The sacrifice of truth.

These are the cards that God has dealt me. To believe and not come up empty. To speak when silence is my nature. I'm older now, and all the bets are in, the bluffs are gone; it's time to show my hand. I'm holding aces and I'm laying them all down.

Confessions
of a
Christian Mystic

I

Into the Mystic

I was pulled into this world one dark night when the power of story was at full tide. Two things were indelibly stamped upon my soul with that first breath: I was born a Southern writer and a Christian mystic.

My mother prayed to die. My army daddy was due back at the base, so the good doctor said it was close enough to my time anyway. To come on in and he'd take care of business. My mother, young and certain of her desire to be a mother, had put on a proper dress and stylish kitten heels, and picked up her purse. She was filled with anticipation and felt fully prepared for the occasion of my planned birth. She was wrong and in for a rude awakening.

The doctor shot up my petite mother with a special concoction of medical syrup, the dosage large enough to birth an elephant. My mother, in such sudden depths of pain, could barely breathe. Could not scream. She would later tell me she felt like she was being drawn and quartered and she just wanted life to be over. She would go on to recount this story to me every year on my birthday.

My father, a gentle man, had been exiled by my mother from delivery. He was teary from her pain, and she was not in the mood for sentiment. Instead, he chain-smoked in the hall. In spite of the megadoses of nasty drugs, I refused to release my hold and clung to the walls of the womb that was my home. My cave of comfort. Surely somewhere in my tiny soul I knew that I was not ready for what lay before me. Perhaps I felt something crucial, one thing, a few cells—or maybe the lifeline on my palm was still in formation. What I thought didn't matter.

The doctor, frustrated with my stubbornness, decided he'd had enough. He grabbed forceps from a tray and fished around until he found my head and clamped down on it without apology. Against my will, without my permission, he pulled me into this earth.

Harsh lights, loud voices. The moans of my mother. Nervous, fast footsteps. My daddy there then, the smoke still curling at his fingertips from a forgotten cigarette as it turned to ash.

My mother held me to her, crying with relief. Her child had come home to her whole from across that great divide. Then she looked at me. My head was slightly smushed, the imprint of the forceps on what would be my cheek.

"That'll pass with time," the doctor said.

A stickler for the details, my mother asked, "Exactly how much time?" Seven years later, my baby sister would arrive in a painless delivery on a Sunday afternoon. My mother told this story every year as well. My sister's face was not smushed, and she had a head full of dark, curly hair. A perfect baby. A painless delivery. She was born a pragmatic child, glued to reason.

In spite of the war of my arrival and all my worthless struggle to be left alone, the night had still been full of magic. The misty kind of bayou magic and backwoods thunder. The palms slapping in the wind, the air tinged with the taste of the Gulf of Mexico. The moonlight trailing from the window fell across the bundle of me bound up tight, and with it perhaps a touch of pilgrim madness. Because the world must have its mystics. Must have its Joans, its Johns, its revelatory. Those who hear voices, mysterious directives, stories that should not be forgotten and must be told.

2

The Dream Readers

*I*n the early years I was cradled and kept by both the hand of God and by a Southern tribe of women who believed in Jesus and could tell the future. The Jesus part was easy; it was as easy as heat lightning on a summer night. They were Southern women, and Jesus ran through their blood like pinesap through the trees. You would think that the nature of God would draw more questions for the telling, more back-chilling, spine-tingling mystery, but this was not my case. This was the black and white of it. The cut and dried. The family Bible on the table. Prayers called out over food and footsteps. Sunday go-to-meeting. Jesus was no mystery; Jesus was real. The future shrouded in forebodings and signs of all kinds—now that was a mystery.

The men in the family knew no future other than the day at hand. They were rough-and-tumble guys. They fished, they worked, they drank. They told lies and alibis. The telling of the things to come was not a part of them. Hard work was a part of them. Alcohol was a part of them. They were made up of three parts survival and one part mischief, so while the men stayed grounded to the earth, to mills and cotton fields, the women were the mistresses of all manner of things. They pulled their shifts, picked cotton, worked peanut mills and water wells—but they were also the keepers of the other things that were a part of life.

They cooked the food and rocked the babies. They tended to all things that fell into their charge and keeping. Blessings and dinner on the ground. Signs and wonders. Dreams and fore-tellings of different kinds. And the women drank this portion of their cup without complaint. Carried the burden of all of it, and the men let them carry it on. Following, slightly frightened by what they had married into.

These mothers of mine, for they were all mothers, could tell things by the weather. By the way wild animals appeared and disappeared. They could call the sex of an unborn child, tell it by the way a woman walked, know if a boy-child or a girl-child was coming. They could find a missing husband cold turkey in the middle of the night three cities away in a stranger's bed. In some cases, they could tell fortunes. For them the veil between time and distance and other worlds was thin, more gossamer than brick.

Like the morning when my grandmother rose from a trou-bled sleep and announced, "Last night I had a dream of muddy water." She paused, took a sip of her coffee from a plain white cup, and looked up.

"Go on," my mother told her. So she did.

"I was standing on a bridge looking for something, looking up and down that creek. The wind was dead and silent, com-pletely absent. The water was full of mud and sorrow. Barely moving."

She looked at my aunts seated around the table, her eyes passing over my head, which barely cleared the table's edge as I sat in my mother's lap.

"I never found what I was looking for."

Then the circle of aunts shook their heads, went to tsk-

tsking with their tongues and picking up a thread of worry. What would come next? A sick child? Dead animals? A husband hurt, or worse? And the worry would continue until, sure enough, the dream would fulfill itself. Bad times would land nearby.

Too small for much of anything but being rocked, I frequently stayed there in that old house and slept alongside my grandmother. A tiny thing lying in that big iron bed, the sound of those old fans with blades that could chop a finger off. Rotating, stirring the hot air. Me, so small with eyes open, still awake. I'd look out the window across the dark field and into the woods. The sole survivor of the day, I would watch as thunderstorms moved across that field toward us. As it drew nearer, thunder would shake the house. Lightning would be upon us until the very air hissed, cracked, and rolled. I thought we were going to die. Yet my grandmother slept on, breathing evenly in and out, exhaling sights unseen over me until finally I drifted off into a hot but peaceful sleep of my own—sheltered there by my grandmother's faith, sleeping as Jesus did in the middle of the storm. The influences of her faith, their shadows, were etched into my bones and into the fabric of my being, emerging years later in stories of darkness and light. Retribution and redemption.

3

The Comprehension of Theological Realities

*I*t was the year we lost it all. President Kennedy was assassinated, and the entire world reeled and shifted with the impact. It was also the day C. S. Lewis and Aldous Huxley died. Of course there were countless other losses that day. Villagers in unknown places. Old people who had lost their memories to a disease yet unnamed. The sick and frail around the world. But all would slip away unseen in the wake of the darkness that was Dallas.

That moment when we sat in front of our little black-and-white television, my mother cried and tried to explain to me, five years old, what had happened and why it was significant. I didn't fully understand the details, but I understood the power of the loss as we watched the funeral procession, the graveside service. John Kennedy Jr., a little man in a suit, saluting his daddy. I already knew about caskets. I understood the stiff upper lip, the straight back.

The death that came the closest that year didn't wear a human face. Tragedy can strike and knock the breath out of you at any moment, whether you are five or fifty-five. My house burned to the ground on Christmas Day 1963. I have spent the rest of my life reeling from the impact. Telling life, "No need to steal my stuff... I'll lose it on my own."

In the wake of this tragedy, I was catapulted into another world. On a jet flying with my mother to Germany, where we would live with my army daddy stationed there. Later, my mother would tell me it was already in the plans. That she already had the passports and had moved the family pictures to my grandmother's. I knew nothing of these plans. So it happened with a one-two punch.

My house burned down. Then I was being taken away from everything I had loved. Now, I think of how young my mother was. Of her losing that little house. Of her roses planted in the morning sun. She was a poor child whose dream had come true in this something to call her own. The fire was fast and furious. Hungry and all consuming, its destruction absolute. There were no charred remains, no recovered precious artifacts of a life once lived. Ashes to ashes. Dust to dust. All proof of our lives lived there locked in memory.

In due time, with age, I could look back and see her as a young, nervous mother carrying me into an unknown country, adjusting to a new life in the face of loss. Putting on a brave face for me. But perspective is potent, and at five all was my loss: The grandmother who adored me, rocked me. The moody South and the sandy-white beaches. Barn cats and wild kittens. Heat lightning and summer creeks. All gone. Replaced by a cold climate where bullies roamed on the base, hid between buildings. Threw snowballs and rocks at the new kid— me. Every day was shaded Shakespearean as I stepped out the door and thought, "*What fresh hell is this?*" in the vernacular of a child.

But hell was still out there on the broken horizon. First, that ride on the jumbo jet, learning of the lightness of being transported, higher and higher on wings of steel. The moment of liftoff when gravity was defied in increasing degrees as we lifted into the sky and entered cloudbanks. A new world unveiled. A white, luscious land of dimension and grace. All my thoughts of cousins lost and left behind were suddenly forgotten as I pressed my nose against the window, searching. I was consumed, devoured by one desire: to see the face of God.

I looked out the window with a steely concentration, patiently, passionately waiting. After a time, I turned to my mother and asked, point-blank, "Where is God?"

"What?" My mother had so many things on her mind. Moving to a country she didn't know. Learning to navigate the waters of being an army wife on a daily basis, not just when my daddy could come home on weekends or on leave. She looked into my eyes the way mothers do when a small child throws them a theoretical ball from left field.

I pointed out the window, slowed down my question as if she didn't understand English: "Where is God?"

She spent the rest of the flight trying to answer me in the best way she could why the entire Kingdom of God wasn't right there, sitting off the left wing just outside my window.

I spent the remainder of the journey perplexed in unhappy contemplation. Where could we go from here? From expecting to see the wings of angels and the face of God to a stewardess giving me a coloring book and crayons—as if that would occupy my mind.

I find it no small feat that not seeing God's face that day on the plane never shook my believing. I discovered that God didn't hang in the clouds just above my head the way I had thought. Concept dead; faith still on board.

On that long ride at that young age I realized that my comprehension of things divine had to encompass a larger territory. The conclusion I arrived at was that the world was larger than my backyard, the beach, my woods. That the dominion of God was wider than the tangible skies.

4

In Primitive Space

I have found the mystical divine in lots of places. I have found it where it has found me. Found it in little country Baptist churches buried so far up the road and back in the woods you'd think it was only the stuff of stories. Found it in open fields where the night sky was filled with those clouds lit up with heat lightning like X-rays. Found it in Georgia watermelon fields, around Thanksgiving tables, in candlelight services, and in a bar talking to an old man over a beer. The divine is not afraid to be present in this life. It's God's wild card. He gets to play it where he wills. And he wills.

Those early days of my life I spent a lot of time with my grandmother. This included going to church with her at the Primitive Baptist Church on the hill. They could afford to pay a traveling preacher only once a month, so that's when church was held.

What the preacher missed in frequency he made up for in volume, in rants and pants, pacing, crying, and crying out. I sat on the front row, head up against my grandmother, secure and safe from the gates of hell with her my certain guardian. When the preaching grew to a shout, when the small congregation piped up with a chorus of *amen*s and *preach-it-brother*s,

I lay down on the pew, my head in Grandmama Estelle's lap. She took those long fingers of hers and ran them through my long hair until I fell to napping, nestled right there in the midst of trials and tribulations, brimstone and hellfire, eternal truths and holy mysteries. The promise of a coming day when Jesus would split the skies, come riding in on a white horse, and change things in the blinking of an eye. I slept on as singing surrounded me, the old women lining it out, laying it down. The white-hot touch of angels hung by a thread in the air on those strange notes.

There was something in that hot, sweaty little church. About those women saying hallelujah, waving their Jesus fans, eyes closed to the fever of that moment. They possessed a piece of God then that I'm still hanging on to, a sweat of passion in the service. They were stirring up the waters of the Holy Spirit until there, among us, settled a peace that passes understanding.

Then it was over and time for handshakes, and "sister" this and "brother" that. Time for "Good job, preacher. That was some fine preaching. Some of the best I've ever heard." The old men gathered their hats from the hooks on the bare concrete wall as the women circled, pulled out dishes. Laid them all out on a long picnic table constructed from a few blocks of wood and a roll of chicken wire. A simple construction made for "dinner on the ground."

Then the hats were off again; heads were bowed for a prayer to bless the dumplings, peas, and corn bread. All the chocolate cakes and two pecan pies. Even then I knew this was an important moment, a part of heaven. The standing together, the smell of out-blessed bounty upon us.

The table sat in the small space between the church and the graveyard, so we settled down to eat inches from the tombstones. A backwoods passel of poor people, hands raised, heads bowed, breaking bread with the living. Breaking bread with the dead. Breaking bread with God.

Years later, those same righteous church folk exiled my grandmother. Her sin was finally divorcing a man after fifty years who had needed to be gone for a long time. But he remained in good standing. Could hang his hat on that rusty nail. Be prayed for and sorrowed over. While she was not allowed to set foot in their midst again. She had been a first-row pew sitter, a true believer. And they broke her heart.

5

Pocketbook Saints

Alice had crow-black hair. She wore cat's-eye glasses, and, although she couldn't read, she was smart in a sensible, country-smart kind of way. If you had passed her in a store, she would not have stood out in her plain dress or her flat-soled black shoes. What distinguished her was when she began to talk: she was tongue-tied. The actual medical term is *ankyloglossia*. I didn't know; I understood her perfectly. And she understood me.

When I was little, my mother worked at an eye doctor's office downtown. Instead of leaving me with the sitter, where I could stay engrossed in *The Lone Ranger* and *The Three Stooges Show* all day, she decided she wanted me to learn things that television didn't offer beyond the realm of *Captain Kangaroo*. To learn how to play with others and be a social child. Enter the Happy Daze Day Care center. It was one of the first of its kind, organized and with verified learning methods that were promised to give a child a jump ahead in kindergarten. I was completely fulfilled at home. I had a television routine. Mornings included *Captain Kangaroo*. Afternoons, *The Three Stooges*. There was imaginary playtime, book time, backyard time, and nap time, and snacks were provided. Now things would change. I had a job to do. I had to get dressed early in the morning and go somewhere besides my favorite rocking chair. In the mornings my mother would take me to Happy Daze on her way to work, but in the afternoons it was Alice who picked me up. All of my time there is a complete washout in my memory. Except for one fateful event and the three days that followed.

We were in the throes of the Christmas season, which meant lots of busywork making decorations. Lots of opportunity for busywork. We were sitting at a little wooden table with chairs; I sat at the end. Being bizarrely outspoken for an introverted child, I raised my hand on this particular day to speak my mind. There were no multiple teachers, no teachers' assistants. My little table was filled with little bodies and faces. There were also three other tables filled with little bodies. Miss Happy Daze had a full boatload. When called upon with a voice of exasperation, I put my hand down and proceeded to say politely, with all the manners I'd been taught, "I'd like to make one of those"—pointing to an example of the thing on a shelf—"but I don't want to make one of those." I pointed to the other thing in a polite but firm voice. I believed in free will even then.

What happened next may have tainted my decision-making process for life. No sooner had the words left my mouth than Old Hideous Happy Daze turned into a witch out of hell. She flew across the room, snatched my waist-length hair by the handful, and screamed in my face, "Why do you not want to make one of those for your mother?" She jerked me from side to side, to and fro, then out of my chair completely. The chair crashed to the floor.

All of the children stared at me in wild-eyed terror. Me crying, which I still resent now, as if a four-year-old little girl shouldn't cry when under attack. But personality is what it is. Showing no pain may be illogical and children will be children, but that woman wasn't worthy of my tears. That's the way I feel now. Then I was shocked and scared, with Hideous Hellion screaming, "What's wrong with you?" while swinging me by my hair. "Why don't you want to make something nice for your mother? You ungrateful little girl."

Eventually, tiring of snatching me back and forth across the room, out of breath, out of steam, her fit passed. She picked up my chair, sat it upright, jerked me up from the floor, and sat me in it. Then she took a deep breath, smoothed out her hair and her dress, and pointed out to the class what an example of poor behavior I was.

The rest of the day in Hell's Hideaway passed with a supernatural quietness. No one asked any questions. Alice picked me up at jailbreak. She took one look at me and asked, "What wrong, baby?"

I lied to her like every other abused kid who fears the repercussions of telling the truth. "Nothing. I'm okay."

"Som'tin happ' in you t'day?"

"No."

Perhaps my legs held red marks. Certainly my scalp did. She took me home, and at the ripe old age of four I sat in her lap as she rocked me without saying anything else about the incident. Without asking any more questions.

It was Alice who drove me to school the following day. She planned it that way. Made certain of it. We reached the Hideous Hideout, but, unlike other mornings, I wasn't dropped off. She parked the car, got out with me. Holding my hand, she walked boldly up the stairs to the door, then bent to ask me where I sat. I showed her, sat in my little chair. She pulled up another little chair from the table, moved it next to mine, and sat down with me, her ample rear spilling over the edges, her black plastic pocketbook in her lap, her fingers firmly on the handle.

Hellhound came over and asked her what she thought she was doing, obviously a little confused. Other adults were never present during school hours. "Can I help you with something?"

Alice simply replied, "I 'tay wid da baby." Those five beautiful tongue-tied words. Suddenly I realized she had known I was in trouble. And that she wasn't going to desert me.

Hellious Helmet-Head was not amused by this. She told Alice she could go. That it was time to begin class. To which Alice repeated, "I 'tay wid da baby."

Hairshredder went all-polite, tried the tactic of Southern grace. She assured Alice, "Everything is just fine. You don't have to worry and you don't have to stay."

To which Alice, stubborn, immovable, replied, "I 'tay wid da baby," yet again. She wasn't asking permission to stay. She wasn't discussing it. She was declaring it.

One last time she was asked to leave, and one last time she answered. Only this time she lifted her feet and slammed them both down in a stomp when she said, "I ted I 'tay wid da baby!"

She stayed. For three days. She escorted me in, pulled up her chair, sat beside me for the entire day. The message to Witch Woman became crystal clear. She was picking on the wrong kid.

I'll never know exactly how Alice knew. Was it my downcast, red, and swollen eyes? My furtive lie? My broken spirit? What matters is that she knew and she acted on it.

My mother didn't find out until years later, when I was a teenager and told her. She was furious at the woman, furious for not knowing. It's probably better that way. She would have done more than sit in the room. She would have pulled that woman's hair out. Not just a strand—all of it.

Then I told her about Alice. About her figuring it out and protecting me.

Most children do not tell of abuse. They are sworn or bribed to secrecy. Or are told they are the ones who will get in trouble, get punished. Now we are more educated about child abuse as a culture, with organizations dedicated to the safety of children who have experienced abuse on many levels. Back then, I just had Alice. And that one ordinary, plain, and simple woman was enough.

We are beautiful, simple saints when we take that one step to protect a child, have the patience to assist the elderly or the love to bear one another's burdens. It doesn't take much of anything but an awareness and the interference of our everyday lives.

My mother lives with me now. She's eighty-six. These days I try to fight her battles for her. Sometimes she still fights mine. Always we try to remember that in love we make room for one another.

I was living in south Florida when I received an envelope from her from back home. When I opened it, one sliver of paper fell out. It was an obituary cut from the local newspaper. The owner of Happy Daze Day Care was dead.

God bless the child.

6

Memento Mori: Remember You Too Will Die

*A*t some point each of us learned of death, and, upon learning, understood that this life is finite in its ways and begs to stay. Not to die. A frantic plea to a powerless mother. Here is my first memory of the dead being dead:

My grandfather's hands are clasped on my sides, tightly holding me in a hover over a casket of an old dead woman for longer than a child needs to hover at two years old. The ghostly face is just under me. My breath can brush her skin, stir her hair if it still stirred. A blood-and-bone Southern girl, I do not cry or scream or squirm. Or yell to be pulled back, put down. I don't even tremble.

We were part of a small group that had come to pay respects during visitation. My grandmother and granddaddy sat on the back pew of the little church. People were taking turns to walk down that aisle, stand at the open coffin. Experiencing the first open-casket funeral in my life was strange enough for me from where I sat with them in the back, but it got stranger when the old man decided my time had come.

My grandmother clung to me, hanging on, whispering, "No, no!" The old man didn't care what she said. He pulled my arm, his hand a vise, and walked me down the aisle at the pace of a bride. A long, slow walk to a black box. All eyes turned on me as I went, every face looking at the child being led one tiny step at a time to face death head-on.

I'll give the old man the benefit of the doubt, light and thin as it may be. Maybe he just thought I needed to face death down at that tender age. To taste for certain the inevitable yet to come. To learn that we were all born to die.

7

Salvation in the Sea Oats

After my mother moved us to Panama City again, she set out searching for a church. She had some criteria on her checklist. She wanted a church where they wouldn't rain down hellfire during every sermon. One where they didn't yell and she didn't have to. One that would allow her children to dance and sing. One that had more dos than don'ts.

At the time, she worked downtown at a drugstore, and one of the pharmacists was the incomparable Barbara Clemons. She was a member of a church denomination known as Episcopal, which was as foreign to us as speaking French. At once it was both strange and wondrous. It was an odd land with practices we didn't recognize, but immediately my mother liked the peace she felt there. The soft way the sermon was offered and the order of things. Now we bow, now we sit, and now we stand. I liked the candles.

After the service, she asked me what I thought. I was eleven, and this is a good age to ask a child her mind. My sister was much younger, so we were going to make her mind up for her. Yes, we agreed, we would become Episcopalian. That decision was made then. Our odyssey to what would become our little home church began. She discovered St. Thomas by the Sea, and

I fell in love with it. It is a small Episcopal church on the west end of Panama City Beach in Florida. It was beautiful in its simplicity. A tiny, white-block church. A white-covered altar, a black cross on a whitewashed wall. Small windows where the actual morning sun would filter in at just the right angle to create a warm glow. At that time, the west end was pretty much still wild. Sand dunes and sea oats prevailed. The congregation was tiny until winter, when all the retired Canadians down for the season came in and filled up the pews.

An old mission bell rang outside to announce it was time to begin the service. When we first attended, a retired bishop in a white robe, with white hair, a white mustache, and a gentle smile, presided over the church, shepherding a tiny flock. It was the stuff of fairy tales. At least in my world. Not a Cinderella rags-to-riches story, or a Prince Charming come-to-save-me dream—but one complete with a mission bell, lit candles, and a priest as grand as Gandalf. It was too good to be real. We had found our spiritual home.

My mother and I signed up for confirmation lessons, which are a part of joining the Episcopal Church. A history lesson, really, about the church and the creation of the prayer book, which is used in addition to the Bible, not in replacement thereof. The prayer book is a collection of prayers, a bit of the psalms, and the services used for such things as marriages and baptisms.

The confirmation classes would spoil me for many things that came later in life. Because the church was so small, the congregation so tiny, my mother and I were the only people who were taking the class. So the classes were offered by the retired priest in his home farther out to the west in what is now the famous stretch of 30A that runs between Rosemary Beach and Seaside, then only an expanse of peaceful sky, rolling waves, and scattered houses. The priest and his wife lived tucked in a tiny house there by the gulf as if they were Santa and the Mrs. down on vacation. He was only mustached and was tall and fit, not portly, but his eyes, oh, how they twinkled. His wife, how merry. Mildred was a dead ringer for the perfect Mrs. Claus. She made us what she called Indian-Russian tea and served it to us with cookies on a tray. This is the most righteous of ways to receive religious instruction of any kind, and I highly recommend it. We sipped cup after cup of Tang-laced tea, nibbling sugar cookies and listening to the rich voice of Father Steele speak to us of metaphysical things like Christ and the Church and living a life of faith.

I was completely and totally captivated. By the priest and his pipe with his soft, thoughtful answers to my questions. By his wife's peaceful presence in the kitchen, the sound of the waves rolling and crashing softly outside, the rustle of the sea oats just beyond the windows' edge. Father Steele had a light in his eyes that was brighter than most. They reflected an eternal wisdom. He had that something I wanted. A surety. As I write these words, it's as if I can see him all those years ago, lighting his pipe with a slight nod in agreement.

It was a long way home from the beach after our visits. We had to travel back up 30A to cross an inlet and then drive from one end of the beach to the other and cross the Hathaway Bridge before we would reach our home in St. Andrews, in an old oak-tree-and-moss neighborhood down by the marina on the city side of the bridge. It gave us plenty of time to talk about our confirmation class conversation along the way. We would review and discuss the things that Father Steele had said about living a life of faith. I was still captivated in reflection, as if I'd been to Rivendell and set among Tolkien's elves gathering the wisdom of the ages.

While my mother didn't make *The Lord of the Rings* connection, she was still journeying into new territory. She was part rebel, part pilgrim, determined to find the best way for her and her own. Which she did. One of the single greatest things she has ever done for me was making this decision and bringing me along on her journey. It was the right place for this writer girl drawn to theology and all things divine.

For the rest of his life, Father Steele played an important role in ours. In all the simple, ordinary ways—such as Sunday-morning sermons that were filled with messages of hope, for communions and counseling, baptisms and weddings—and in the moments when life became too dark to bear. When our uncle was murdered in cold blood, my sister's nightmares were constant, dark despair. Then, with a listening ear and a soft word, Father Steele somehow healed her, delivered her. It's no small thing to touch a child's life that way. It sits right up there with the Acts of the Apostles—taking a hand and saying, "Rise." From that day on, she slept at peace again.

Many years later, my father would emerge from the jungles of Vietnam alive, but scarred in ways we could not see. This small-town backwoods creek boy would get baptized in the same manner as my sister and I had, with holy water held in a giant conch shell. We would begin a Sunday ritual of a family going to Sunday service followed by going to breakfast. It didn't last forever, but it lasted for some years. My father and I never shared that trapped look here, as we had when forced into those Easter clothes and made to pose for a photo op. He smiled in this new place. Shook hands and sipped coffee after the service. Maybe smiling is a good barometer for knowing if you are in the right place. And that the people you love feel welcomed and at home.

8

A Shot of Jesus and a Snippet of Truth

(A letter to a spiritually minded author friend who is confused by Christianity of the Southern variety)

Dear Kaya,

About a hundred years ago you wrote to ask me about Jesus. How it is that Southerners seem to know him personally. Asked if they felt that gave them absolution for everything. Forgiveness at their doorstep. I wish there was an easy answer.

I know you are of another mind than what you might perceive as Southern Christianity. However, I also know that you are one of the most honest, pure people I know with deep spiritual resonance. I'm certain that Jesus knows that too.

I have no easy answer for the other. I was born believing in Jesus. I'm a Trinity girl all the way. Explaining the faith of other Southerners would be something I'd be hard-pressed to do except to say, yes, Jesus gets personalized in such a way that he becomes a friend to all. Savior to some. But it is not the religion that media or most movies portray. It's as variable as the individual. That's always been God's wild card, if you ask me: the card of free will.

Lately, I've been reading Flannery O'Connor's letters and her prayer journal. If you have read her stories, then you know they have bizarre ways of exposing the darkness. That they sure can exemplify the evil or meanness in someone. They also do it in a delightfully funny way. Not everyone likes her. Maybe some Christians don't like her work because of that dark belly of some of her stories. I can understand that. But if they had read her letters or her journals, they would know her heart to God was all consuming. She labored over those stories. Cried for God to inspire her and make her words the right ones. She was a true Southerner and also a devoted Catholic. Her spelling was possibly worse than mine. Her brilliance far greater. In some ways I might relate to Flannery more than anyone in that literary way we search for our heroes. I am Southern and Episcopalian. Devout in my ways as she was in hers. A writer of stories who can be both amusing and touched by strange things that are not religious.

On your question of Jesus and all that forgiveness: sometimes I have to work through those things as well. Like Flannery, I feel that, in writing fiction, I don't sound pompous about these subjects; I just let them unfold the way they are supposed to. Let the characters work out their own issues with forgiveness and damnation. And they do. But, also like Flannery, I fear that when I write in an expository fashion it sounds pompous as hell. "Inflation lurking around every corner," as she puts it. I wish she were alive today and we could sit down together and discuss some things. Her prayer journal is such a jarring introspection of her heart to God. Her concern that what she wrote be a good story and one of which I guess she hoped that God would approve, not in spite of the violence or humor in some cases, but because it was the story that came through her. The one she had to tell.

I so understand that, and I think you do, also. We distill down our personal experience to its core elements, the DNA of the story, from all we've ever felt or heard or tasted for ourselves. All those raw elements becoming something that will then rise in the form of story but fully in its own shape, the characters of their own making. I've been working for some years now on a novel that rolls in the Southern gothic tradition like mud. Religion and life get combined into a literary mash-up. The title is The City of Truth, *which I think Flannery would have approved. I've included the prologue below. I think it will help you understand where I stand on all that sin, absolution, forgiveness, and God—which is to say I fully believe and am as mired in the muck of life as everyone else. Sometimes the greater truths lie folded in the lines of the stories we tell. Or our greater truths. The things that are most revelatory. So the easiest way for me to answer your question is to illustrate in story rather than get all kinds of pedantic, to which I have no right.*

The City of Truth

Prologue

The night they strung my granddaddy up from the hanging tree is one of the most memorable ones of my life. Not because of all the shouting or even the thunderheads rolling across that dark, daring, empty field, but because I was not the least bit afraid. I had the greatest sense of peace about me. Even in the midst of what I was old enough to understand would result in the end of a man who possessed much of my memory. It was as though I knew, come what will, God was on the throne in heaven, and the women were on the throne of Truth, and nothing else mattered. My world was secure, and so was I.

Now the men were there too, shuffling their feet in the dirt and saying, "Aww hell, Ruth," under their breath, but they didn't count much. They're not what I remember so well. When you are surrounded by wide-hipped women bearing shotguns and full of enough righteous anger that it would split the hairs of angels, you don't consider that too much argument makes good sense. After all, a hanging tree generally has room for another customer in due time.

So there I was on the night of April 16, 1962, when they sat Granddaddy on Buford's horse Old Tom with his hands tied behind him. He didn't say much of nothing on account of it wouldn't have mattered. Not a bit. He knew it too. He also knew that he was guilty of a heinous crime and had sinned against his own flesh. If you have decided to pick up sin at any time, sinning against your own flesh is not the place to start, but it could very well be where you end.

Old Tom looked a little skittish, which was understandable considering he was used mostly for plowing and occasionally for fun, but he had never been called upon to serve as executioner. It was a new experience for him. For me too, seeing how I'd never been to a hanging before or since that great, fateful night.

Ruth yelled out above the noise, "You got any last words worth saying?" Granddaddy opened his mouth to speak, but I think his throat was too dry to muster words. Daniel, my oldest first cousin on Momma's side, yelled, "The word says, 'Vengeance is mine, saith the Lord.'" And Ruth hollered back at him over the wind of the storm,

"That's the word, all right—there's no denying it. What you need to understand, Daniel boy, is that I'm serving as the Lord's assistant." Daniel couldn't help looking at things like he did because he was under the calling and grew up into being the first preacher of the city of Truth.

So Daniel read a passage from the Bible while the horse shuffled his feet back and forth, and then Granddaddy tried to say something or maybe swallow. I couldn't tell which. I have yet to understand Daniel's choice of passages. His voice rang out with a great, powerful timbre, as a voice does when it's under the calling, and he described in detail the beheading of John the Baptist and how his head was then brought in on a platter and given to the dancing girl, who gave it to her mother. I don't believe it gave Granddaddy a bit of encouraging news. Maybe in the end Daniel just wanted him to know that he was in good company and that sometimes even the saints of God came to a terrible end.

The wind shook the long branches of the old oak, all the way out to the ends, and the rope around Granddaddy's neck swayed back and forth like it was part of the old tree itself. With a spit on the ground from Ruth followed by a spit on the ground from all the other women, the men removed their hats, Ruth fired her shotgun, and Old Tom took off. The rope snatched out straight and Granddaddy lost that hump to his back as his feet tried to find ground that wasn't there. Then Ruth said, "That's that," and everybody turned to go as she commanded, "Don't you dare look back." I didn't know if my mother was speaking to me or the company in its entirety, but I locked my eyes on Aunt May's rolling-thigh shanks as she took wide steps back toward the city limits and what we considered civilization.

Lightning shot down and into dry dirt to my right, so close my hairs stood up on my arms, the back of my neck. When it struck again I heard that lightning lash out, make a crack, and the sound of a limb with a hanging man come crashing down. Even at nine years old I knew there were times you never look back. This was one of them.

So, Kaya, you can see that things are not as neatly packaged around here as they might seem. I daresay that what is most prevalent in the South is our predisposition for story in all its forms. Our skeletons in the closet are so numerous we can't even shut the door. We just invite them to pull up a chair and sit down to dinner. If there is anything that connects us more than Jesus, it is the story of Jesus offered to us from our parents and grandparents and theirs before them. It is an assumption and assimilation of that comfort that comes so easy we tuck ourselves in at night knowing Jesus is there. It's some kind of powerful glue that I cannot deny. Christianity in some spheres of the North or out West when I lived there seemed more controlled. A box within a box within a box. In consideration of the Southern Christian and our Jesus—it strikes me that the sap that runs through the lifeblood of that belief is more akin to the Native American hidden power. More shaded by superstition. More alive with the power of the unseen being very, very real.

I have come to terms with this fact, the conundrum of the Southern tradition. Where the dangerous side of God might be more easily felt in a tiny backwoods Baptist church than in a dignified Sunday service. And like the storyteller of Truth, there is no turning back for me. This is where I belong. Where God remains in the danger zone. And believing has never been too sane or simple.

I think it's the human element that we string from a wire. Think Flannery again. It's the human element that is a dark underbelly of the story of us. Jesus is good. Human is up one day and down the next. The forever odd element that will move the story forward.

Peace to you, soul sister. Send me your words.
River

9

Mark Twain Has a Twitch

Joan of Arc heard voices, so people called her strange. Her accomplishment in leading armies and saving France has stood the test of time, so her strangeness has been justified. It's Mark Twain who strikes me as strange. This cantankerous, agnostic, wooly-bully author of the ages was more than a bit smitten with her. He was obsessed.

The only book my parents ever took turns reading to me was *The Adventures of Tom Sawyer*. The storyteller with the quick wit and wild hair was compelled to study Joan for twelve years before he wrote what he considered his greatest work, *Personal Recollections of Joan of Arc*. It's very cleverly written as a memoir by the Sieur Louis de Conte and translated "out of the ancient French and into modern English by Jean Francois Alden." All Twain. If smoking and drinking exist in the afterlife, the man in the white suit with the white hair is having a scotch cocktail, smoking a cigar, and laughing his literary head off.

At least I like to think so. That when he crossed over whatever portal he was walking into, he saw door number one and door number two and was able to say, "I hear Saint Joan went this way. I think I'll take my leave and saunter after." Slid in on the coattails of his years of research and serious dedication.

This afterlife might be a shaky concept where Twain was concerned. Atheists love to claim him on their lists of celebrities, but I have my doubts about his doubts. His quotes on Christianity seem to be on religion's abuse of man, and on man's abuse of religion. They are a touch angry. Where there is anger there is usually fire. And where there is fire, passion. Indifference is another thing entirely. Mark Twain was a lot of things, but being indifferent is a quality never attributed to him.

He was so proud about the Joan of Arc novel that he became frustrated when readers were perplexed by the fact that it was serious. It just wasn't the funny they expected of him. They wanted America's storyteller to come back to the fireside, lean back, and give them a good tale about a frog-jumping contest to bring them to laughter. He was great at that. But the man had a scratch named Joan, a young girl willing to sacrifice everything based on a divine directive.

The opening of this Joan of Arc novel is lacking in wit but possesses such poetry and fervor that I wanted to quote it for you here. Then I realized I was typing the entire foreword. It's easier to tell you to access the book, which is in public domain now, and read it for yourself. Twain spent a dozen years studying someone so devout who believed in God and angels, in whispers from the divine, and who inspired a country to fight and an army to win. And, as if winning wasn't enough, she inspired those soldiers to be more moral, to aspire to virtue, to recognize the Holy. For twelve years he studied this sweeping history—and lived in the mind and soul of "Saint Joan," as he referred to her.

Joan believed with all her might in that divine source. Twain believed in Joan. The line between the two is so thin it's the stuff mystics are made of.

IO

The Timely Art of Inspiration

*I*n the year of my birth, people were reading everything. Television had not taken hold to the point of one hundred fifty-two channels twenty-four hours a day. There were no cell phones, no internet, no social media. Understandably, other forms of entertainment thrived. Literature, theater, and the movies found a solid place in society.

So there was no shortage of every genre from Southern gothic novels to mysteries, fluffy romances to historical fiction. The classics, of course, always. But there was also the introduction of the work from a new-beat generation often fueled by drugs and road trips. What people wanted was a good story, and they got it.

There were so many stories being read that I can close my eyes now and still hear those pages turning, like waves—steady, certain, finding their way to shore. All those people before me. All those stories. Dancing in and out of the shadows of light and time. All those readers finding their way to the final page, the final line, the final word.

Capote had *Breakfast at Tiffany's* and Chandler ruled with his good guys who were always on the edge of being bad but still managed to save the dirty day. A time when the dames of those stories wore skirts and had great gams, when men wore hats and were snappy dressers. All of it added up to a kind of dark-night-in-the-city sultry I would come to love.

Our very own Southern boy, Tennessee Williams, was a literary rock star. *Cat on a Hot Tin Roof* had won him a Pulitzer, and now it was hitting the big screen. It showcased Taylor, Newman, and Ives with so much heat pouring off those words that steam would rise from the silver screen. Beckett's *Endgame* had just taken the stage in London, and twenty-five years later I'd be sitting in the dark theater, watching rehearsals of *Endgame* and *Waiting for Godot*, where humans melded with words and brought them through character to life.

Irving Stone's *The Agony and the Ecstasy* was released to great reviews and would be the first book of which I would truly be in awe, realizing that it was more than a novel; it was a thing of beauty written about one of the most divinely gifted artists the world would ever know. I read those words and wandered through the days of Michelangelo's imagined life.

These stories all became a part of the art of inspiration that fueled me forward, integrating into my life in sometimes odd ties and strange ways. Because I believe God uses the art through image and word to send messages across time. The divinely inspired work of the Bible. The living water of a word in due season whether it comes from a line in a play, a scene from a movie, a chapter, or a chapel ceiling.

Julia Cameron illustrates this so beautifully in her powerful work *The Artist's Way*, which validates the spirituality of the creative act of storytelling. What captivates me is the power these works have to withstand the test of time, to continue to communicate across generations, as well as the universality of the message. I take away what I need from a story; I see what I need in a fresco. You take away and see what you need. I consider this a sublime touch of the supernatural—contained in inspired art. I value it greatly and yet can sometimes get in my own way during the creation process, hammering away at something when breathing into it would be the better thing to do. I must remind myself that it is by divine inspiration that the good story is told. That the holy muse is a trustworthy muse.

When Michelangelo included the Greek sibyls, the images of the prophetesses of old, on the Sistine ceiling, it might have seemed a peculiar choice. There are the prophets of old and then the sibyls. Perhaps he intended to balance the male and female aspects of the story he told visually. The history of the sibyls is easily discovered now through a quick search, but suffice it to say that they were considered ancient oracles who stood in the sacred places and communicated by divine inspiration. Later, they were embraced by some Christian factions as having basically always foretold the coming of Jesus.

Some years ago, I was banging my head against the wall, asking God what to do with my writing. I can't even remember the reason for my angst now, only that it was pressing and it seemed paramount that I receive an answer. Later that week I attended a communion service. It was a simple, small noonday affair in the middle of the week. Those services are usually not very well attended, so there is a quiet intimacy to them that I value greatly.

During this particular service, the priest, not given to offering any type of prophetic direction, said, "For some reason, today I just feel like if you are seeking an answer from God for something, today is the day that you will receive an answer. I just feel this strongly." Well, that is certainly a beautiful setup for having one's expectations on the increase. But later that day I received an answer that satisfied me in the way of misdirected mail.

I had been renting the house I lived in for many months,

but on this day in particular, when I went to the mailbox, I found a postcard sent to someone who must have lived at my address previously—someone who was long gone into the unknown. It was a postcard of Michelangelo's *Erythraean Sibyl.* The text below the picture said that this sibyl brought the message that God would come into the world in the form of the word and communicate with man. Mailed from Italy. It was all the answer I needed, because it brought me a peace without comprehension. I didn't know exactly how it applied to me, but I felt certain that it did. Although it had been mailed from someone in Italy to someone who hadn't lived in my house in a year, I believed that for all practical purposes I was the one it was intended for all along.

Years later, and not so long ago, I would stand in the Sistine Chapel and look up at the image of that sibyl, thinking of Michelangelo, of *The Agony and the Ecstasy* that was his life. Of how his story and his art had found their way into my life and inspired me. My cousin Deb bought me a beautiful, large, framed print of the same image that now hangs over my fireplace, a reminder that the divine muse is eternal and speaks to us all through history and across time.

11

The Last Dance

S*aturday Night Fever* hit the screen, and John Travolta had made it cool for guys who worked blue-collar jobs all day to comb their hair and dance all night. There he was. All jiggly strut, swinging that paint can in one hand, catapulting disco into the mainstream of America.

It was a time of contradictions. Erich Segal's *Love Story* was a hit, but so was Stephen King's *Carrie*. Ditto for James Dickey with *Deliverance*. And William Peter Blatty had a hit with *The Exorcist*, which would soon be produced and hit the screens, driving most of us to keep our bedroom lights on for eternity.

Donna Summer sang a controversial song that was recorded on one full side of an album, *Love to Love You Baby*, which became a sensation. Everyone thought they looked cool because we had moved into the seventies wearing Izod shirts and jumpsuits. The sixties had ushered in bell-bottom jeans and tie-dyes. Disco gave us polyester, and a primped-up look that flipped the coin on being laid-back. Coke became the drug of choice. Pot was smoked just to take the edge off that coke-induced zoom.

At the time there were lots of nightclubs in Panama City Beach. There were nightclubs that promised you could party with thousands of sweaty people wearing different perfumes, bouncing and grinding, the heavy scent of titillation and desperation all wound together. All those words put together now make me feel itchy and claustrophobic.

But for a season I partied right along with them because I was young and stupid and thought I was having fun. Given a do-over, I'd study foreign languages, work as a journalist writing novels in my spare time. Somewhere in there I'd work in reading to kids. If I'd only known then what I know now. I'm older and wiser and realize that every moment in life is precious, and all that partying in the end became something else. It was like riding a beast into the jungle where it gets denser and darker all the time. I was never riding the beast at all. It was leading me into the darkness, to eat me one bite at a time.

In the height of that disco craze, people twirled on the floor, a silver disco ball above them with ever-changing colors. The flash and twirl of the dancers was so beautiful, but it was fueled by the wrong things. In the midst of all that glitter and glam, the undertones of desperate bled through. Eventually, the harder the bodies twirled, the more the underbelly of loneliness exposed itself for what it was.

Final call and closing time brought on "Last Dance," a closing song for all clubs—rock or disco. After all these years, I can still clearly see that crowd. "Last Dance" is just starting, and the remaining faces shift; as the lights begin to lift, all eyes begin searching, looking for someone, anyone, to make the night last a little longer. To put off the light of day and whatever it has to say.

We fought off the sunrise because the new day would pull back the curtain of reality. As long as Donna Summer kept singing, we were all flying high, searching constantly for someone, something, that would complete us. The secret was to keep twirling beneath those lights, to continue hearing the beat, to pour all of our passion out into those dark hours, because when morning came we would be alone with ourselves. Wake up just who we were. And that was never enough.

Years later, I looked out to discover a familiar face as I was doing a reading at Davis-Kidd Booksellers. It was none other than the disco queen herself, Donna Summer. She possessed a calm, a confidence, a surety. She invited me to lunch, and we went on to have lunch together a couple of times before she passed away. We exchanged other books. She brought me a copy of her memoir and wrote a note inside. It's one that stays on my to-keep shelf. She also brought me a copy of *The Other Bible*, which includes the gnostic gospels and other texts. Donna was looking forward to our discussing it at our next get-together. Unfortunately, the world lost her to cancer just as our friendship was blossoming. We had both come through other seasons and found a place in God and within ourselves. We had drunk from the water at another well.

12

Mad Dog Jack

*T*he messengers in my life have come in all shapes and sizes. Have sometimes been sent in strange ways and on odd days, when the dark was all encompassing. Sometimes they were as tiny as that postcard. Other times, as perfect as Father Steele. He looked the way you would expect a heavenly messenger to show up: regal and dignified.

Then there was Mad Dog Jack.

To tell that story, I have to begin at the beginning, because jumping to the end builds no proper foundation, no understanding of the importance of just one honest conversation. And of a kind of trust that only comes from knowing and knowing very well.

I have no idea where the Mad Dog nickname came from, although it might have been left over from his service in Vietnam. When I met him it was through an act of kindness and (I suspect) a touch of pity. A high school friend looked at me one day and said, "I need to take you somewhere to meet someone."

Anne was the kind of friend you often have in high school. One you know from ringing bells, stories, smiles. From shared classes and hallway chatter. I'd never been to her house, and

she'd never been to mine. We didn't share a bus or a neighborhood, so our contact was in passing but always nice. I
remember that her smile was always warm, and I felt that she
accepted me for just who I was. The pity was due to the fact
that I had a haircut that looked like a helmet. One my cousin
and I had received at the same time from someone who was
someone's aunt who had decided cutting hair would be her
trade, no training required. Maybe she had shaved poodles before she hung a sign and bought a hair chair, the kind that goes
up and down. It was a one-woman, one-chair shop. Up until
then, we had been teenagers with long, straight hair.

How we found this lady I do not know, but, unfortunately,
we had. The thing that still astounds me is that my cousin
went first, and I watched as her beautiful golden strands were
whacked and gaffed beyond recognition. She stepped out of the
chair, and I should have run as the woman lit another cigarette and said, "Your turn." But I didn't. Like someone willingly
walking up the stairs to the guillotine and laying her head on
the chopping block, I stepped into that chair and sat down,
fully knowing what was to come. Me and cousin Deb were just
that close. We still are.

The result was that we ended up with identical cuts. It
looked as if the woman had run a lawn mower over a layer of
our hair, leaving the ends long all the way around, but on the
crown of our heads sat a cap. A literal cap, only made out of
our own hair. We went back to the old neighborhood where all
the kids gathered 'round us and began to laugh, saying, *You got
a cap cut; You both look just like you're wearing caps; You look so
stupid,* and other supportive things like that.

So this monumental day of mercy arrives, and Anne drives
me as a surprise to a salon in her part of town. There were
many chairs and many stylists, but she walked in and requested
Jack. So self-assured—I remember that about her, about that

moment. Me standing there, out of place, and Anne a rock star, taking center stage.

"I've got someone I want you to meet," she said.

Out walks Mad Dog Jack. Tall, lean-legged, wiry, with dirty-blond hair. He ran one hand through my hair. There was a quick assessment, and as he smiled at me, the edges of his eyes wrinkled into lines. An appointment was made and Anne delivered me back to school.

When that appointment arrived, I was on my own. I sat nervously in the salon waiting room with other women, still feeling out of place. Until I took my turn in that chair. The rest, as they still say, is history. It's silly to say a haircut can change your life, but it did.

In fear and fascination, I watched as he lopped off inches, quickly cut layers fine and sure, the hair cap on my head disappearing. Then he gave me my first real blow-dry, in quick brushstrokes. He was in command of this ship, and there was no doubt in his mind that he was doing the perfect thing. He was so convinced; so was I.

I emerged a different person. Somehow a confidence surfaced that had been sorely missing. I wish I could buy awesome, life-changing haircuts for everybody who needs to see himself or herself in a better light. I wish I could find another one for myself.

The amazing thing was that that person was inside of me all that time. The same little girl who raised her hand in that day care class to voice her opinion before she was attacked was the girl who was now resurrected and looking back at me from my reflection.

Seven years. That's how long I returned to that chair. Every six weeks, rain or shine. That's a lot of chair time. I watched his business explode, multiply, and get out of hand because the demand for him went viral. During that time I went from being a shy piece of the wallpaper to someone who dared, come what may.

That man was a sculptor, a wizard. He could look at a woman, just look at her, and see who she really was. What shape, what color, what cut would move with the texture of her hair. What would showcase something unique and special to her that no one else possessed. That's a divine artist. It's the way that God sees us. Our beauty at our best, now and always.

At some point, after all that time, I wandered off and began seeing someone else. It felt like cheating, like I was sneaking around. He was a new guy from New York. Smart, quick-witted, gifted too. Such a rare breed, but now there were two of them. By then, high school graduation was a fading memory and I lived alone.

It was that time of Donna Summer and all-night parties. From time to time, in passing, Jack would show up at my door just to say hello. He had forgiven me for seeing this new New York hairstylist. For changing things up. But by then he was an old familiar face. He was my friend.

One afternoon I was hanging out with a girlfriend when Mad Dog dropped by. We were having a serious discussion about *The Lord of the Rings* and what an amazing piece of work it was. We were hanging out, drinking coffee. Black, straight up, and strong. In the middle of all that, Jack says these words: "I'll tell you the truth." He paused a moment. "You'll never be happy without Jesus."

I started laughing. There was no disrespect meant in that, but it was about the equivalent of watching Cheech and Chong in *Up in Smoke* and one of them saying the same thing. Slowly it dawned on me that Jack wasn't laughing.

"No, I'm serious," he said. I could see that he was, and I changed the subject. Then we talked about absolutely nothing memorable until I walked my friend out, said good-bye, and sat back down.

Then I leaned over and said, "I'm sorry. You were serious and I didn't mean to laugh at you. I honestly thought you were joking."

He shook his head side to side and said, "I'm not joking."

I'd known this man for a long time. Seven years is a lot of moments and conversations. And I knew that if he was saying this, if he was seriously saying this, something had happened.

"Tell me about it."

He stood up. "I can't or I'll start crying." Then he started pacing the small living room, and as he paced he told me his story. And this is where sometimes, being a writer, your fingers freeze on the keys. Because you want so hard to explain things the right way. You want so much for someone to understand your friend and to honor what he said in this very private, very personal moment. You want so hard to get it right, but you know you'll get it wrong no matter what you do. That you'll never be able to convey it, so you simply do your best.

Jack told me this:

He was home alone. He'd just bought Linda Ronstadt's new album, *Just One Look*, and he put it on and lay on the couch listening to it. But then the needle on the turntable contin-

lifting and dropping on that one song instead of playing through the album. Then he told me that he had been brought to his knees three different times. Now he began pacing and crying, deeply. He was trailing a roll of toilet paper I'd given him in one hand, saying, "I told you I'd cry!" He continued talking about this vision, about seeing heaven opening up and seeing Jesus. Still crying, he said, "It's like I was getting just one look. That's all. Just one. And it's so hard to live your life another way when you've been living it so long another." And he went on and on about Jesus and some other stuff about heaven and the devil.

Eventually he calmed down. At least he stopped crying. And then he left. But he had started something whirling within me. This whole Jesus thing. I had gone to that little church with my grandmother; I had been raised in the Church for the most part. I had spent those weeks with Father Steele and knew that what he had said was solid gold. It's not that I didn't believe, because I did. But this was something different. Something close and personal. Something haunting. The fact that it was coming from this dope-smoking, skirt-chasing, wild man I knew so well made it all the more haunting, because it made it more real. If someone else had shown up at my door with a canned speech, a pamphlet, and some Sunday invitation, no matter how well intentioned, I wouldn't have received it. But from Jack, I knew it was the truth.

I felt something pulling, like an undertow going out, but instead of pulling me out to sea, it seemed to be pulling me to the shore. I had been affected. As if not Jack but Jesus had come calling. So instead of going out the next few nights, which was the standard thing to do at the time—to hang out with the posse I was running with—I decided to stay home. In the morning I sat on that little plastic sofa in that small living room and drank coffee and thought about stuff. And I sat on that little sofa at night and had a glass of wine and thought about stuff. And at some point in my thinking, I said that Jesus prayer that Christians are famous for testifying about. The kind they try to get other people to say so that they can cross over into the pearly gates without hesitation. But it wasn't fear that brought me there, just like it isn't fear that keeps me.

I don't know anything about those pearly gates—who's at them, in them, or on the outside. I can make all the glorified assumptions I want, and the only thing I'd trust is that they might be wrong. But I do know what I do know. That when I said that prayer, that little *Jesus, here's my heart* prayer, in that private moment, something happened. I didn't walk to no altar, didn't answer no call, didn't get caught up in a wild tornado of Holy Ghost Revival. It was just something personal, and private, and real.

I started staying in at night, and when friends called and said, "C'mon, where we going?" I told them I'd be staying at home. Told them they were welcome to come by for a glass of wine if they wanted, but I wouldn't be joining them in the loud melee those years had become.

A kind of peace settled over me and in me that I hadn't felt for a long time. Not since those days at Father Steele's. His pipe smoking. That Russian tea brewing. The sea oats rustling.

If only I could have hung on to it without letting it go. Kept myself right there on that track. But I didn't. I went slip-skidding away. It's what some people call *backsliding*. I can't really argue with them. I think, as a matter of fact, that I have to hand it to them. That's pretty much what it is. It wasn't that I didn't believe that moment was real, that I lost my faith along the way or anything close to it, because I did not. What I lost was a sense of me. A balance. A kind of self-respect. And self-respect is crucial to being healthy. Particularly at a young age when you are bombarded with peer pressure and influences that seem to overwhelm you. As you get older, you learn; you can pretty much say *that's not for me*. But even then, the appeal of being liked, of being one with whatever group takes the day, the desire to be included, or simply the desire to be loved by your mate, can be overwhelming, a long, dead-end road.

It takes a lot of guts to keep playing your own song when people are laughing or throwing darts your way. Our souls get weary of defending ourselves for anything. For watching what we watch, for drinking what we drink, for believing the way we believe. Or for not watching what everyone else watches, or not drinking what everyone else drinks, or believing the way others don't believe.

Here's good old Shakespeare again: "To thine own self be true." Which doesn't mean to step all over people. It simply means find your truth and follow it. And don't assume it's what you want it to be, either. The easy thing. The fun thing. The simple thing. The opposite of what you've had all your life because you just want different. Be still. Be quiet. Listen. Then follow.

I saw Jack only once more in my life. It would be years. I'd find him to cut my hair on the day I had my second child. Getting a haircut was on my list that day, but it wasn't to look great or to find myself. It was to get it out of the way so I could focus on giving birth, then caring for an infant and a toddler. I sat in the chair and watched Jack work. He was in a small shop now. One on the beach. A shop he didn't own. And it wouldn't be long before he'd leave town again. But I got the chance to tell him how much his story had meant to me. How it had affected my life for the better and forever.

He was older, tired, still struggling with those lingering demons. He nodded his head when I told him this. Closed his eyes a moment and looked away, trying not to cry. After that I went years and years without knowing where he was or thinking of him often. Until I did. Then he was on my mind in a sudden, obsessive kind of way. I asked around. No one knew where he was. Then someone said they heard he'd gone to Atlanta. It was still the prehistoric days where we wandered aimlessly without cell phones. We lived in a search-engine void. I called information, searching for his name in the Atlanta area code. Nothing.

Not too long after that, I heard he'd died. Not a great death. More a just-gone-downhill-for-a-long-time death. He'd had his "just one look" of heaven. The curtain pulled back for him as he was brought to his knees. It may have not perfected the way the man lived, the peace or the grace that was readily available to him on this side of the line, but I'd bet Jesus that grace and peace and mercy were waiting for him when he crossed over to the other side.

13

Emmet Tells a Story

When Jack had paced the floor crying that day as he told me his story, I had received every word. Sometimes I'd paced alongside him, the toilet paper in his hand spinning out, trailing in a white stream. Such raw, honest emotion. And such a powerful experience.

It is difficult as a writer to capture any moment that involves this type of supernatural. I can just imagine Jack trying to sit before a typewriter and share this story on the page. The thought process becomes stagnant. The words are never strong enough or soft enough. Nothing about it seems possible to convey. The words become stilted, flat lines that mean nothing.

This is one of the significant reasons why telling those deeper truths is such a treasure to me. The brushstrokes are different, the essence of the story told with a lighter touch but stronger surety. In the fiction I feel I get it right. As if a painter, brush in hand, is moving under the instruction of a loving master, as, for instance, in my short story about Emmet Gainer. He experiences a transformative moment that renders him speechless.

The Light at the Window

Emmet Gainer was a man of solid reputation and serious mind. He was not one given over to mystery. To the mumbo jumbo that threatened to pull every third man he saw under. He was determined to keep it that way. Better safe than sorry. Who knew what tomorrow would hold? What kind of crazy could come upon them? Better for a man to know how to hunt and eat than to stand there on the corner waiting for someone to hand him a fish. Hand him a spear. He didn't need anyone to hand him anything. He took what he aimed for. It was hard work. It was always dirty. It was never fun. And he wouldn't have it any other way, because bygones were not bygones. Bygones be damned. It was about survival and he aimed to.

Emmet was not a praying man, because he was not a man who believed in much of anything beyond the borders of his reason. The tides of the moon he knew. The miracle of dirt and seed and harvest. But all that was unseen, and he was most comfortable with that which stayed out of sight.

He was of a company of men who considered themselves self-determined. Not those clinging to the old notions of deliverance and hope. Of kingdom come. He walked the earth with a stomp and a roar. Even if no one ever heard it, he did—and that was all that mattered.

Or that was the way it all had been forever and always. Wasn't nothing but one good day. That's all. One simple day of good work done and coming home with a meal set. A simple meal of stew and meat. And he was enjoying it the way he always had. A good meal was a good thing at the end of a hard, long day. The chatter of a baby girl a sure thing, the soft pat on the shoulder of his wife as she passed behind him to finally take her seat. All of it. Just as natural as the day come along.

Then that light got caught in the curtain above the sink. It was normal light first, but then it wasn't. It took him a little while to notice. His glancing first, then returning, time and time again. The sunset he knew, the casting of the last strong rays before evening come. But as he brought the spoon to his mouth, once, twice, nodded to his wife although he hadn't really heard her, his eyes stayed focused on the light—unchanged light. It was as if the curtain had caught that stream of gold just between the parting cloth and held it.

He grasped his iced tea, the glass cold from the beading of the ice along the outside, wrapped his hand around it, and took a slow sip. Emmet stole a glance at his daughter; the light caught her hair and she was pure glorious. The most beautiful thing he'd ever seen. Goldilocks, he thought. And he would call her Goldie then all her life. Her name had been Rachel until that moment, but that would never matter now. He would call her Goldie even when she was older. Even when she cut all her hair off in a rage at her boyfriend. And on her wedding day when she had grown it out long again.

His wife reached out, patted the back of his hand, said something he couldn't make out. Maybe asked if he was all right. The light, he tried to say, but the words didn't quite form as he had intended. He looked at the window again. The light was tangible to him now. It was a thing that knew him. Knew his courage, knew his fear, knew his every pain and promise. He had stopped eating. He had forgotten his hunger.

His wife's name was Emily. She was a woman pretty

in a simple way, of simple means. Her smile held a world of patience. She patted his hand again—her hand cool on top of his—and every time she touched him he felt such tenderness toward her that he teared up. He looked down into his stew to avoid her eyes. A tear fell straight down, landed in the bowl. He clutched his spoon, an ancient tool, as if he could carve his way back to his natural world. A quick glance up. The light—it hadn't changed.

His hands were like old clumps of roots of those big trees. Blistered, raw, and gnarly. They were the working hands of a serious man. He had swung them once at a man. He thought he'd killed him. Never swung no more. Never had to.

Some old man had said, "Emmet is a knock-'em man." He had punched his right into his left palm and laughed. "With just one swing he knocks 'em to the ground."

That was a long time ago, but the fear of a man with hands that swing like clubs had kept him safe. No one would suspect how deep the tender ran beneath his dirt-stained skin. But his wife, his girl—they knew.

The girl was telling a story, the mother smiling, nodding. He smiled too. Only catching bits of sing-song voice. The words didn't matter to him. He was in his chair at this table sitting with his simple family in a simple place. A steady, sturdy world.

But now, there was the matter of that light. Unshifting at the window. Unnatural.

Then, in the hushed tone of confession, he spoke: "He's come to me as light and mystery."

His wife followed his intent stare. She saw nothing but the white curtains above that kitchen sink. The girl turned, followed her father's face, and, seeing nothing, turned back quickly, asking, "What is...?" but before she could complete the question her mother laid a finger on her lips, caught her eye, whispered, "Shhhh." Then they sat in a church-like reverence, silence enveloping them, neither speaking nor eating but waiting for the man to say something again. To do something. But he did not. Not for quite some time. Until slowly, with blinking eyes, he turned his head and looked at them. The spoon had been clutched all this while, and he now gently rested it in the bowl. Then he lifted those large, scarred hands up to his face and wept.

It had been something he never spoke of to anyone except his wife one night late in bed when all was silent. He had spoken to her in whispers, but his voice was deep and heavy. They lay in darkness except for a sliver of the moon's light that escaped the window shutter and made its way across the room, spilling onto their bed. He tried his best to describe the color of that light, of what he saw and what he felt, but he didn't try for long because he couldn't make it right. "He came to me" is all he finally said at last.

In this way it seems the telling of all the miracles in the world is not beyond reach. The actual illuminating of them in such a way that a man could sit down, take off his hat, and realize— that could be me. I could see me in Emmet, and if it could happen to him, that moment of light, it could happen to me. And in that moment of reading, it does happen to those who are carried along by the words. We become shape-shifters all. We do indeed live a thousand lives through a thousand stories, but what's more important to me in the telling of them is that the reader is able to experience something, for all of life and what's beyond to be real in that single moment. The magnolia opens, the rain falls, an old prayer seems suddenly heard and a heart revived. Such is the beauty of language. The power of story. The perfection of prayer.

14

When First We Learn of No Tomorrows

(A letter to a granddaughter on death and living a resurrected life)

Dear Ella,

I was thinking of you the other day. Not just as you are now, a beautiful young woman, but you as a little child. Someone I have loved for a long time died recently, and that brought to mind the time when you first learned of death. That is the time you fully understood it. The perceived finality of it left you weeping. You asked your mother if she would die, and when she replied yes, you were beside yourself. But then dismay became horror when you asked, "Am I going to die?" She answered truthfully but assured you as best she could that you would not die for a long, long time. Safe to say, it wasn't the answer you'd hoped for.

Not too long after that, we were on a road trip. Just me and you driving through the backwoods of Georgia on some state highway. The trees were green and shadowed the road, and we had reached a stretch where there were no houses or towns—just us and the green in the late afternoon. It's always magic, that dappled sunlight. You loved to ride with the windows down and to listen to the radio. That was all you needed. No noise or movies then. No cell phone or Snapchat, Facebook, Instagram. We were actually there in that moment together, fully alive. Which may be precisely what sparked you to turn to me and ask, "Zaza, can we just stay here forever?" Those big blue eyes, filled with tears. I was so taken by surprise by the question that I asked you if you wanted to stay in the car. Then I realized it was more than that. It was the indescribable moment of being present in this life. Fully possessing it. I did my best to say, "No, not exactly, but we will always have this moment with us. This time, the light, the warm air. We'll carry this forward with us forever." That satisfied you well enough for us to go on.

It is unfortunate that time goes by so much faster than we think. Certainly faster than we realize when we are young and given to feeling so immortal. The secret, then, is to respect the moments that we have. I was brought up in the company of some serious people who worried a lot.

At a very young age, when I perceived the reality of death, like you, I was horrified. I turned to my mother and explained that I didn't want to die. Perhaps that is a commonplace occurrence. When your uncle realized that aging greatly increased the chance of dying, he declared he would have no more birthdays and that was that. He accepted the gifts but not the sentiments declaring he was getting a year older.

When I was little, there was a large family of raconteurs of a few generations. Someone was always dying. Death was always around, prowling like a hungry dog, never seeming satisfied. It is this awareness, in many ways, that pushed me ever closer to that edge between believing or not believing in an afterlife.

That old Southern family of which you are a part was something akin to a large Italian family from the movies. The rituals surrounding our people who were sick or dying. If you haven't already done so, I'd encourage you to read The Book Thief. *The story is told through the eyes of death itself. Death, as the narrator, becomes a character who mourns the loss of life even as he must take it.*

Now that you are no longer a little girl, it is normal for you to question how to live the years you have before you and what to believe in. You may decide very much what you believe and then change your mind from one thing to another. To test the waters of what you've been told with what you discover for yourself. In due season, I would hope that you find a faith that is true to you and a comfort there. A safe place from what life can throw you, because, even in the best of times, being human can take its toll. In the worst of times, that faith can be the center of your being and all you're hanging on to.

I pray that you find a resting place, then, in yourself. Where your faith can grow for all your days. I would hope you can grasp the other side of that coin that is death, which I believe is resurrection. All these are words that may matter little to you now but someday echo back in ways you long to hear. I encourage you to live with a courageous and fearless passion the life that you've been given.

Loving you always, my Ella, from here and beyond,
Zaza

15

Signs and Wonders in Ordinary Time

*I*t's Easter morning. What better time than this to confess of signs and wonders? Strange things on ordinary days. If there be any mystical moment in the history of the faith of Christianity, it would be resurrection. That life could exist beyond the tomb of death, which all men fear in the silent chambers of their hearts. Not the fear of dying as much as of ceasing to exist. The possibility of all loving and all knowing disappearing into a sea of nothing.

Resurrection. What greater sign from God than in the midst of all our trials and tribulations there is a seed that will germinate, burst forth, and live again. Signs. Wonders. I once had a message that I would have a visitation from God. This came to me in the innermost place of me, that same tone announcing holy visitation in the way that a thought about an item you must pick up from the store comes to remind you: don't forget the milk. The same way that Anne Lamott described Jesus following her around like an invisible stray cat in *Traveling Mercies*. So I had received this word, visitation, along with a sense that indeed I had something coming.

I had been helping my cousin out a few days a week at her coffee shop and had spent the night with her in Panama City, Florida. This promise of a visitation weighed on me more like a threat of haunting. I slept with the light on, which means I slept very little. I kept telling God not to just show up and shock me. Not to suddenly appear at the foot of the bed. Not to walk out of the closet. The list of *not-tos* went on and on as I dozed fitfully until after dawn, when I felt this sneaky-in-the-night-visitation thing had been laid to rest. Thinking that surely God, like a vampire, wouldn't dare show up after sunrise.

As I drove the next morning to my Airstream, where I lived in the woods, this entire story unfolded. I laughed aloud at my ridiculousness. I have craved seeing the face of God since earliest memory, since that plane ride to Germany when I was five, my eyes searching out the window for this being I believed in. I laughed at the absurdity of my fearing what I longed for. More than that, at my telling God precisely how he could and could not reveal himself. Right then and there I struck a bargain, made a declaration—out loud—while I was driving over the big Hathaway Bridge that spanned the bay and the open waters to the gulf.

"Who am I to tell you how to present yourself? I'm sorry. Forgive my fear, my simple humanity. Show up anytime you like, God. Show up in any form or fashion. Dead of night or noon of day. Just show up, please."

That night it dropped below the freezing point. The tiny propane heater cast just enough warmth for a tiny spot. I had lit a small candle, an ordinary candle, the kind you might pick up for a quarter. I had placed it in a holder sitting on the little table and lay down on the floor, where it was warm. Watching the flicker of the tiny flame, I fell to sleep. Sometime during the night I had a visitation—

nothing like I had expected and stronger than anything I had yet experienced.

I woke up lying there on my back looking at the candle flame, but the light, the fire, had been replaced by something else. A golden orb, a circle, floating where the flame would be. This is not your ordinary gold. This isn't something earthly. It is the goldest of gold. It makes the word itself unworthy. It moved lightly as if a breeze circled in the room. This would be a sufficient sign in and of itself. But no, in the midst of that gold was a triangle shape with three white dots like stars resting in the sky. They were joined by a line that completed the triangle. This image hung there in the gold. It was *my* image. The one that I have doodled for years upon years. Father, Son, and Holy Spirit. The Trinity. I imagined myself standing, sitting, living from that center point in the Trinity. On troubled nights, I'd look up to the sky, seeing so frequently three stars spaced in perfect balance one to the others, forming the triangle of my trinity.

This was my visitation. My reaction was a deep, abiding peace that makes no perfect sense. I said something like, "Cool"; then I rolled over and went back to sleep. I woke again to a heavy peace that was as thick as the fog that rises from the valley below my hill. A peace so deep there is no space, no inch, no molecule of room for the tiniest worry, the fretful thought. Still the symbol hung in the center of a gold so rich it is a glory in itself. *Oh, it's still here,* I thought, and rolled over and went back to sleep.

Once more I woke and there it was, still hovering. I watched for a while in this unnatural peace, said, "I get it, God. Perfect balance in the fire," and rolled over to sleep again.

Later that night I woke once more, the apparition gone, the candle flame returned. I noted it as nonchalantly as if it happened every day—"Oh, it's a candle again"—then I blew out the flame and immediately went back to sleep.

The morning came, and when I woke up I remembered everything in a state of manic panic. "Oh my God! I've had a visitation. I've been with God, a thing, this symbol hanging. Gold, super gold, floating gold. And I went back to sleep! Perfect balance in the storm. What kind of message would that be? Or maybe that wasn't the message at all."

Later someone asked me why I didn't take a picture. It never occurred to me. Why I didn't touch it. It never occurred to me. I wasn't seeking scientific proof for what I saw. Although now I understand why those writers of the Old Testament and New Testament would say, *Whether in the spirit or in the flesh I do not know.* A pastor told me later that year, "No one would have seen that except for you. Anyone else would have simply seen a candle flame." I hadn't given that possibility any consideration. Until then. Was this what the prophets talked about? Would Moses's bush seemed to have been burning to others, or did it only burn for him?

I saved that tiny butt of the candle for a long time. I lit it the next night, wanting God to show up again. But God doesn't perform parlor tricks; his presence is not cheap magic. That peace, in and of itself, was a gift, helping me to realize this is what it's like. This is what Jesus spoke of. The peace that passes all understanding. That gold so wonderful, so alive. The white dots, the lines, the symbol. Perfectly mine. I realized that God meets us where we are. That our individuality is his creation. That thing about the number of hairs on our heads—that's not much, in light of this. He knows the workings of our mind, the bending of our heart. And our true soul longings.

Never again. No midnight surprises. No other visitations

that break through boundaries of that dimension into this one. I wanted to save the candle, encase the thing in glass. But I reminded myself it wasn't the candle that was holy, sacred. It was the one who used it. As he uses us; as we are used in glorious, mysterious ways beyond our comprehension.

16

A Sloe Gin Fizz and the Myers-Briggs

One of the things I love about fiction is all the different worlds that we can experience simply by turning the page. That deep variety of authors who take their personalities to the page and then allow all the personalities of their characters to emerge and take the stage. Ann Patchett's lovely, adored classic, *Bel Canto*, is a perfect example. Rarely can an author move through the waters of characters so effortlessly while giving the reader a sense of inhabiting that skin, that life, that breath. It seems so effortless in the reading of it. *Pathos*: the deep feeling of sympathy or sorrow as such a person feels the same pain. The understanding of one another. When we are moving to different drums. Remembering that we are still of the same dance.

If all the characters dance to the same beat, speak in the same tone, the story becomes a bore. In this life we will never become boring. In all of God's great creation the variety of us, the awesome multitudes that we are, is a never-ending fascination. There is the adage that opposites attract and the truth that like-minded souls spirit one another forward. That deep calls to deep. And seeks both understanding and answer.

Defining ourselves and others, though, has passed in and out of fashion. The Myers-Briggs test became and still is one of the most commonly used personality tests. Major corporations rely on it, as do counselors, who utilize it in couples counseling. It was introduced in 1942 by an unlikely source—a mother-and-daughter team with no professional training or degrees in psychology. The test gained in popularity with the general public, owing to the fact that, unlike other tests, this one wasn't fashioned to pass or fail. It was simply an indicator of where someone fit on the scale of being extroverted or introverted: more analytical or feeling. Todd Essig writes in *Forbes* magazine that the personality test remains a mystery in spite of its popularity. Obviously, the validity of the results is not why people embrace it so much.

Enter any party in the early 1990s, and the Myers-Briggs Indicator was more talked about than the body mass index in later generations. The 1920s had the flapper; the 1990s had self-diagnosed celebrities. The test represents the identification of self and finding the tribe of your dreams, one that accepts you as you are. Even the outsiders long to belong.

In the playing out of all those moments, here's a little something I call "Gin and James Dean":

❧

There's a buzz in the room that would sound like a hive of bees if you weren't looking at the people, laughing, chatting, cigarette smoke rolling in at a regular pace. The throttling hum running through the room is fueled by all the regular alcohol, but with an extra thrilling of a theme. Come as one of your famous Myers-Briggs personality types so that people can guess your identity. This makes the party intellectual and sexy. Filled with the flaunt of self-discovery.

I'm wearing a black turtleneck and black pants, sipping a gin and tonic, standing on the edge of the crowd, watching. A woman surprises me at my side. She is glittery. Very. She takes in my black on black.

"Well, have you had yours done?"

"Had what done?"

"The Briggs."

I watch her sparkle, take a sip of my drink. She took this reflective pause as confusion on my part.

"You know. The Myers-Briggs personality test. My results were so amazing. They just, you know, got me." She pulls a long, thin, brown More from her bag. "So have you done yours? You know it's what we were supposed to do before we came tonight."

"Actually, I did."

"Did they tell you who you were like?"

"You mean if I take after my momma's or daddy's side?"

"What a scream. You're such a joker. I bet your test told you that."

To the guy walking by wearing an overcoat with his collar turned up channeling James Dean: "She's such a joker, Eddie. Do you have a light?" Eddie does.

"Thanks." One long inhale. "No, what I'm saying is what famous personality are you supposed to be?" She takes a long sip of her drink and decides I'm not at all who I'm supposed to be. "Well, what type are you? Do you know that?"

I play along. "Oh, that. Well, yes. I float between an INFJ and INFP, depending on what season I'm in."

The shiny lady smoking a More takes another long sip of something pink and tells me I'm missing the point of the whole party. It's not about who you are, but who you are supposed to be. "But who are you? What famous person are you like? You can tell a lot about yourself just from that. Guess who I am?"

She poses, shimmies, purses her lips. Decides I'm too slow to play. There's a sparkle in her eye when she says it, a little bend and dip to her knees, a sway to the hips for emphasis. "I'm Marilyn Monroe."

I nod. "Of course you are." I consider the ramifications of being a sex symbol.

"Now, honestly, tell me who you are."

I decide to play along.

"Joan of Arc, martyr, fifteenth century. Counselor Deanna Troi, *Star Trek: The Next Generation*. Yoda, *Star Wars Episode V: The Empire Strikes Back* in the saga against Darth Vader."

She pulls on the cigarette, inhales deeply, and exhales. A Morpheus cloud of smoke hangs between us.

"Oh well." She looks into her drink glass. There is nothing there. "You can't always tell about those tests. Oh look, there's Randy. Woo-hoo, hey, who are you?"

And she's gone.

Not everyone wants to hang out with a martyr or a little green thing that talks in riddles. Particularly when they are in their heyday of channeling Marilyn. They don't fall under the fun, let's-go-party types.

A personality test I once took pointed out that my personality type made up only one percent of the people on the planet. The test went on to explain that the only things I wanted were (a) to save the planet and (b) to be understood. That's it. Save the planet. Be understood. A simple day. It went on to explain that the chances of my being understood are minimal, considering I'm part of a personality type that makes up one percent of the population. Which could work to my advantage because not being understood can force someone to walk straight out into the desert for a soul-questioning cry of *Who am I?*

Which is precisely, exactly, divinely when God shows up to answer.

17

On Rumi and the Tongues of Angels

*T*he wind today rattles the house. The doors shake in their locks, desiring to be opened, rattling at the door frame. The chimes swing and call out; the birds are happy with official spring. I listen to the wasps and pretend they are the buzz of bees, so relaxing. The house in this season is morphing into what comes next. It is a far cry from where it's been. Only fitting that it was as broken as I was when I returned. It was empty, waterlogged, abandoned. We were both in a state of loss. The rains and the vermin had taken their toll. Both of us were bruised and battered in ways that went unseen until the structure was laid bare. Nothing can be left alone, unloved, and thrive in the absence of that attention. At least not most things. And the monks who are cloistered away are basking in their time with God, so they are very much not alone as it seems. They are conversing in the caves of God.

Rumi the Sufi poet captures more of that breath than any other to me. Recently, I indulged in a purchase of *The Essential Rumi*. From the first page, he leaves me breathless. The all completeness: "In your presence I don't want what I thought I wanted." My mother says she doesn't believe in praying in tongues. That is, she doesn't think the experience authentic. I think she finds the sound of it disturbing after her experiences of being in a place where the spirit rained down a river and the people broke into shouts or dances—began to speak in other tongues. To her, in that midst of wild was some type of crowd disorder. The people were just getting all cooked up or something.

"I speak in tongues," I tell her. We are in the car at night, late, on the road home from shopping. "It is a language, not babble. Inevitably, the interpretation of what I say is something that is my deepest desire or longing or expression. It is something that gets to the root of what I'm feeling deeper than anything I can voice in comprehension."

She is silent. Surely I have mentioned this to her before, or maybe she is hearing it for the first time at eighty-five—her very Episcopalian daughter confessing to her in the tired, dark hours of driving. An easy time when my eyes are on the road, not her reaction.

"This is not some gift that fell on me in a mass hysteria. A friend explained it to me this way many years ago: if I want to pray for someone but I don't know them, I can just pray in the spirit and I am praying exactly what they need." So that's what I asked for Mom. A year after that conversation with my friend I was at home, alone in my prayer time. And that's what I received. "It's not a parlor trick."

I pull into the driveway to the house. The driveway is long and dark. I've forgotten once again to turn in that signed request for a safety light to be installed. The house is dark as well. We haven't left a light on, imagining we would be home long before the sun set. The lights from the car catch the outline of the trees, toss shadows backward, away from us in our approach. I pull up beside the house, turn off the car. I think of praying something, an illustration. "When I pray that way it sounds like a language, Mom, because it is." Again, I think,

Just pray. Show her. But did Rumi need to prove his truth? Did Leonard Cohen need to show his magic? Instead I open the door, get out of the car, and help her inside.

Then I return to the car and unload the groceries. One trip after another. I hate doing this in the dark. Mom offers to help; I tell her no, it's okay. Really, I have this. My back is tired, my shoulders slumping. Some days it all seems never-ending. On my last trip out I stop, look up at the stars. Then I lean against the car in the dark and keep looking up. That sky, those celestial objects light-years away and right above me. They are my shortcut to God. At night I look up and find myself like Rumi, realizing I don't want what I thought I wanted. To explain the mysteries that can be explained but never understood. I breathe in that light from above, carry it into the house, let it turn to seed and scatter.

18

The Happenstance of Ghosts and Other Matter

*L*eonard Cohen has been following me around. It's not a haunting, not exactly, but there he is again. It began simply, my hearing "Hallelujah" played and the refrain clinging to my brain. Residing there and never moving on. So that, waking or sleeping, there is Cohen. On a Sunday walk in a grove of trees, there is Cohen, singing "Hallelujah," a blaze of light in every word.

I manage a few days to get away and write. When I arrive at the small cabin, there are only two books. One of them is by Leonard Cohen.

A few days later, I turn on the radio and it opens in the middle of a discussion with an intelligent, fascinating character I'd love to know. At the break, they announce, "We'll be right back with this recording of our last interview with Leonard Cohen." Of course, I say aloud, *What are you telling me? What are you pointing to? What am I missing? What message is supposed to break through the ether now to lead me on?* I'm still trying to comprehend what God is trying to show me through this would-be monk-poet. Like a message in a bottle, there is something there for me to find and discover. I'm still searching for that answer. Somewhere, between the contemplation of time, matter, energy, gravity, and multiple realities, I'm sure I'll find the answer.

It's similar to my interest in theoretical physics. This from a girl who barely passed algebra with a D minus. Yet, in spite of the nausea of those moments, how lost I was in class, and my rational incomprehension, I am as attracted to $E = mc^2$ as a bear is to honey. Fascinated with the possible realities of time travel. Not in an H. G. Wells time-machine kind of way, but more in the manner of "time is relative, as each moment happens continuously." The movie *Arrival* was based on a short story of the same name by the brilliant Ted Chiang in which aliens arrive on the earth in an effort to keep us from destroying ourselves. Their communication illustrates how time and memory are more circular in motion than a chronological, flat plane. That time is indeed relative.

One of the theories of theoretical physics is that we live in but one universe in a multi-universe existence. If all physicists of the world will look the other way, I will explain in my words, in my limited understanding. The concept begins with the big bang. The power of that moment was so mighty it continued echoing expanding energy, which formed other universes potentially made up of exact copies of all life—including us. Maybe that is not even close to the right explanation. But it works for me. There are singular-universe theories and multiple-universe theories of various manners. One version is that, in this alternate universe, the same versions of us have the freedom to make other choices along the way. To take the other road. To marry the first true love, take the job in California, move to Spain, invent that thing, pursue the holy grail.

Last night, at home, I was downstairs watching an old recorded episode of *The Big Bang Theory*. I went upstairs to ready for bed but turned on the television there so I could continue listening to the show. The television downstairs was still playing because I was completing all of my night chores, locking up. Upstairs and down, I thought I would be able to listen to the show as I moved about. However, when I turned on the television upstairs, a current episode of *The Big Bang Theory* was playing. Two different episodes not related to one another were on at the same time—the same characters and same structure of reality but with different story lines.

Just prior to watching *The Big Bang Theory* I had been watching the Science Channel. It was a special show on the explanation of multi-universe theoretical physics. As Spock might have said, *Fascinating*. So I found myself standing in my bedroom at a pause, experiencing two different realities happening at once—albeit with fictional places and characters, but a perfect example.

In one of the episodes, the character Sheldon Cooper is desperate to get tickets to the new *Star Wars* movie on opening day. When it appears all the computers are locked up and they will not be able to get into the site to purchase tickets, he declares it's time for drastic measures. I expected a quick, illegal brainiac hack of the system to acquire said tickets and laughed aloud when he dropped to his knees to pray, saying, "Dear God, I have never believed in you but you know my momma. And if you can get me tickets..." at which point the character Rajesh declares, "I'm in." And Sheldon continues, "And I still will not believe in you," and gets off his knees. I might have written that episode a little differently. To me it was God who got Rajesh in, and Sheldon's prayer had been answered faster than he could finish the words. Perception is everything. Sheldon is funny. His momma is funny. He is serious about physics. She is serious about Jesus. I love the story, the physics, and the *Star Wars*–, *Star Trek*–, comic book–obsessed geeks all the characters portray, only I wish, at some point, Sheldon had a moment where the power of physics did not negate the presence of God. Where the beauty of science and the metaphysical could meld.

Dr. Francis Collins, who served as the head of the Human Genome Project and is currently the director for the National Institutes of Health, in interviews and presentations with PBS, CNN, and National Geographic, among others, made a great case for why he is a man of science and of faith and how the two are compatible.

The late Dr. Stephen Hawking had a brilliant mind, and at one time he was a declared atheist. I loved Dr. Hawking's sense of humor, evident in many of his lectures, interviews, and guest appearances on *The Big Bang Theory*. After his older brother, whom he declares to be a rational man, had a near-death experience, he changed his mind, at least to some degree. I believe the universe is as large as Dr. Hawking said it is. One physicist said that there was definitely an intelligent creator behind the work of all creation and that it was the work of a master mathematician. I agree. Somehow the building blocks of all matter possess an exquisite message. Somewhere along those stardust discoveries are the clues to our origin and destiny. I think that in due time all those mysteries will unravel to show a thread that leads straight to the heart of God. One who loves us and desires our company in the midst of the vastness of all that is. Which makes it all the more mind-blowing.

19

Kung Fu Communion

*L*ast night Mom and I watched *The Forbidden Kingdom* with Jackie Chan. This was quite by accident in a channel-surfing kind of way. Before we knew it, we were caught up in the great choreography of many fights happening simultaneously, some of which required flying through the air. It looked like a great amount of dedication had to have gone into becoming a super-natural martial arts warrior.

There have been great courses of time when I was walking with God in an old-television-show, kung-fu kind of way. I didn't lose my cool. I didn't lose my peace. I was plugged into something greater than myself to such a degree that I operated from that place. Moving by the spirit was my first reaction, not last resort. I have been known to do this for months on end, thinking of this great creator of our existence first thing and last thing in my day.

When I think of people who were spiritual legends in their own time, the Smith Wigglesworths and Mother Teresas of the world, I imagine that they did likewise. The man who said he never prayed longer than fifteen minutes but he never went fif-teen minutes without praying. The woman who said that deep down in every human heart there is knowledge of God. And deep down in every human heart is the desire to communicate with Him.

Legend has it that once there was a gathering of pastors at an event, and Smith came to pray among them. The presence of God filled the room and grew stronger as they prayed. The report was that each man stayed for as long as he could but eventually left the room weeping and fearful. Smith was the last man standing. He didn't leave. Later, a pastor revealed to someone that as a matter of pride he was determined to stay, but in the end he could not. He said that he felt if he had remained another moment he would have died.

It's the kind of story that's easy to toss away. The kind that pairs well with an eye roll. I'd have to see it to believe it. Except I have seen it. I have experienced just that. It happened at a large international prayer gathering. It was a women's Aglow conference held that year in Orlando at a place that would accommodate women from countries around the world.

Tommy Tenney was there to give a keynote. He had authored a book titled *The God Chasers*, which had become a phenomenon. It was his testimony. He spoke about chasing after God more than anything. Desiring the palpable presence of God. I don't think he was praying when this happened. He was simply speaking—calmly, not hellfire-and-damnation preaching like the pastor from my childhood. Just talking in a normal tone of voice. Then I heard a cry begin far to the left of me in this huge convention center. The sound was the weeping of hundreds of women suddenly moved to tears. The voices gathering other voices as it moved. The wave was headed my way. Then it hit. I don't remember weeping, although all the women around me now were weeping mightily. Surely so was I. But it isn't my own tears I remember. The lasting impression is my thoughts at the time. The simple knowledge that now I will die. The flesh will melt from my bones. I would turn to bone and then to ash. Not from fear. Not under the arm of a mean and spiteful God. But because this presence is too divine, too strong, too powerful for a mere mortal to withstand it. I knew this felt inevitable, and I was not afraid. *I shall die today in the presence of God,* I thought. So be it unto me. Then after some time that presence lightened, lifted, and was gone. The vacancy of that space was still warm to the touch. Women were still crying, but quieter now. A hush fell. An awe. We had shared more than an experience. It had been an encounter.

If Smith walked with God like that daily, then he was certainly more able to bear it. To live and breathe in the presence of the divine. I haven't obtained that and might never do so.

I go to church. I seek the lost, serve in my own way. Light candles as I pray to ask for things for myself, my family, my friends, and for strangers. I am genuine. Yet something troubles me. I have caught a glimpse of what lies beyond the great divide. Experienced the supernatural. Still I become swamped by realities on this side of that veil. The distractions that weigh so heavily on my mind and heart are things that are so temporal and passing, be they perceived small or large. The mortgage payment or that broken thing that must be fixed. The extra pounds put on, the goal to take them off. The dog or doctor. My heart sometimes broken, sometimes healing, all sometimes on the same day. Everything a distraction from that which I know to be true.

I wonder what it would be like if everything was put into perspective. If the words "Seek first the kingdom of God" shook out in my life, what would that look like? In my version, at my core, what is my answer to that? In my image of that I am happy, not living up to other people's expectations, not seeking the approval of those held dear or those whom I don't know. My question to myself, then, is, What will it take for me to lay aside the sins that so easily beset me? Conversing on social media before listening to God. Peeking at the headlines before I write. Allowing a thousand demands to swallow my gifts and callings whole each day until I'm gone. Bartering with God with these gold coins called time.

There is a table that awaits me within my soul. If I will but sit, be silent, and turn my thoughts toward the one who waits. The only thing a true mystic wants when the earth of our circumstance crumbles away—the union of communion.

20

On Mystics and Sexual Healing

*I*t's a late night on the bay in Panama City, Florida. The old oaks are stately in the darkness, the Spanish moss swinging in the salty breeze. It's the kind of setting I take for granted, but should you arrive here with no experience, you would look out across the water at the tiny boats, the lights of the dock, a restaurant named the Shrimp Boat hanging there by the water's edge, and you would say, Paradise. You would be right. I'm sitting with a few friends, females only this evening, and so it is a females-only conversation. Things I might not discuss but certainly have friends who do. In the midst of all this, talk about sex, work, life, and sex again. At that point the conversation was leaning heavily on the topic of having a healthy sex life and exactly what that entailed, and a friend turns to me out of the blue and asks, "Exactly what do you consider a mystic to be?"

Conversation came to a stop. Everyone looked at me. Great question.

The word *mystic* conjures up all manner of things. Images of wizards and warlocks, perhaps. Gandalf and Galadriel for those who find their magic more of the

Middle-Earth variety. It's understandable that there is so much confusion surrounding the word. The dictionary itself seems confused.

I have a worn-down, binder-broken, highlighted-page, old copy of *The Reader's Digest Great Encyclopedic Dictionary*. It suffers a great need of being rebound before I lose entire letters of the alphabet. While I use several dictionaries for cross-referencing, this one has served me better than others. Yet even in my beloved broken copy, the definition of *mystic* seems too far ranging. It's as if the lexicographer was grappling with all the possibilities. Here, a mystic is something of or pertaining to mysteries. There, something designating an occult or esoteric rite. Or one who believes in or professes to have had mystical experiences. And one who participates in mystic rites.

The following definition of the word lines up more appropriately for my use: *Mystical: of the nature of a direct, intuitive, or subjective perception beyond the ordinary range of human experience, especially one of religious character.* Also, having a spiritual character or reality beyond the comprehension of human reason. (As Einstein reflected, believing the world was flat was just good common sense.)

There doesn't seem to be one definitive answer to what the word means. So it's left to interpretation and understanding in relation to the person associated with it. There have been many mystics throughout history. The Catholic monk Thomas Merton was considered a mystic. The Sufi poet Rumi also a mystic. Evelyn Underhill's book *Mysticism*, a classic first published in 1911, explores the facts, traditions, and examples of mystics so thoroughly I wouldn't even attempt to add a word to that body of exquisite knowledge. Suffice it to point someone to Evelyn Underhill and say, "If you have questions, read her work."

There are Jewish mystics, Sufi mystics, Greek mystics, and from what I hear tell a Cherokee Christian mystic living somewhere down in Tucson. The mystics were people who could find that place where they could reach if not the hem of God's big train, then at least see the radiance of it that reached across the stars. They had this wild desire to find some piece of God to hold on to. Find God as if it were like going home. Not as if they were trying to discover something new, but more as if they were trying to get back to something they knew long before their birth.

They were priests, nuns, writers, and everyday people. Some of the mystics hung out in the desert, some worked in stores, and some walked the streets. They lived on mountaintops, in houses, communes, and caves. Maybe for a good portion of their life they were busy doing something that looked rather normal. Say, perhaps, like shooting dice, watching reruns of *Gunsmoke*, chasing women, or catching men. But then they woke one day with a hunger for a true north for which there was no name.

Nothing, then, could satisfy. No great concert, no wedding feast, no new love, no distraction or accomplishment could satisfy that hunger in their soul. They sought and sometimes found. Then lost ground, that holy place they had managed to touch slipping through their fingers. Then, as true mystics, they began again. This dance of searching, catching, finding, losing. This Song of Solomon, waltz of lovers. My lover is my life, my everything. I wait for my lover; I want my lover. My lover is at my door, but I missed the knock. I opened too late. My lover is gone. Where is my lover?

And those people, the ordinary mystics of the day, are still around. They are authors and desk clerks, songwriters, lawyers, bartenders, teachers, cowgirls, and more. Their souls have been stirred to seek. They're not always so obvious. They could be the person on the bar stool next to you or a neighbor down the street. Mystics don't usually announce themselves. Especially if they have seen some things out of the ordinary. Then there stands a good chance they could be labeled as crazy. Mystics are safe from the distance of a hundred years. Like a cozy mystery, from the pages of history there is nothing to fear. But up close mystics could be crucified, drowned, or burned alive for telling the truth.

I have kept my own cards, my experiences within my faith, close to the vest. Hidden. Safe. Private. I can be most comfortable not stepping foot outside my house for weeks. Not uttering words. Not speaking on the phone. In silence. Writing from a room from a safe distance. Me, here; the world, over there.

But God doesn't create us to stay in our deserts, our houses, our private places. There are the cloistered, the prayerful, and they have their special place. I believe in the beauty of their work, these nuns and monks who stay recluse and pray around the hours. I call upon them, submit requests, am comforted by the knowledge that they are behind the walls praying day and night. It is their calling. But not mine and not most of ours. If all the world were cloistered, we wouldn't have each other.

So, unguarded, I find myself sitting around a table with women drinking wine and posed with this question. One that asks what I consider a mystic to be, but the bottom line is that question is also asking me to define myself, my brand of mysticism.

I am a Christian mystic. My belief and personal theology is devoted to the Holy Trinity of God. All of my mystical experiences are seen and experienced through that truth. The Christian part has been with me all of my life, through all of its stages. So has the mystic. For a long time I didn't want to claim that word for fear that it would be misinterpreted. Also out of a sense of respect for the famous mystics from the likes of Hildegard to George Fox. I felt the title of mystic had to be earned and bestowed. That in being awarded you had to be legitimately recognized by a well-renowned theological institution. For the sake of official titles, for instance in the Catholic Church, I'm quite certain this is true. Officially, to be recognized there is a checklist of the verification of this and that. In the writing of this book, I had to come to terms with the fact that I am what I am. If you are very fortunate in this life and you live long enough, you get to the point where you finally, fully, accept your identity.

So what is a mystic? The women are watching, silent, expectant.

"Someone who desires to live and breathe and move in the presence of the divine."

There are head nods of assent. "Okay," someone says, "I can go with that."

Just like that, the word has entered and exited the conversation. More wine is poured and the conversation returns to sex, work, and the pressures of life. To politics and vacations. To our children and the future. To our lofty goals, aspirations, and creative endeavors.

When we walk outside to say good night, there is that long, sweet pause of lingering. We lean on the car, look up at the stars and across the water. *Truly, this is a piece of paradise,* I think.

My friend says, "The house is always open to you, River. Come stay and write. Anytime. Whether we are here or not, I'll leave a key."

Over the years there have been so many friends with open doors and open hearts. I bless these people as I come and go. I pray that for every peaceful place they have provided me, peace and blessings fall like rain on them. That the residue of any good thing I bring with me will remain long after I am gone. The mystic in me does that. In the end it's the most substantial, trustworthy part of me that I know.

21

Full Moons Cast the Longest Shadows

I have watched the moon coming and going since I was a small child. All these years add up to so many moons. Tonight, the moon hangs low and heavy, a pregnant woman ripe with lush, new life.

I live on a hill where the trees are very tall. In the quiet of this full moon, the shadows of these trees, their leaves carved and waving like dark silk against the ground, captivate. In the midst of life changes and seasons changing, I am still surprised by this. The moon. I lean from my window like a lover pining for a beloved, one quick glimpse never enough to fill me. In winters my face is pressed to the glass; in summer the window is up, my screen off, so I can lean on propped elbows and, like an old grandmother watching children play, take my time as shadows shift and move. Catch the glimpse of the huge wingspan of an owl.

The full moon wakes me, stirs my soul to sleepy window-watching always. Tonight it is winter pushing into spring. Warm enough for windows open, branches bare enough for stars to fill the sky, hide among the passing clouds, then emerge again.

My heart opens up in thankfulness, a prayer I toss out to

God. For this, this beauty of this night, this moon, these trees, those stars, I thank you. Such a simple thing, a thankfulness. Then the flood of peace that fills me overflows.

There is so much peace I cannot contain it. I am full of gracious bounty. I pray that this peace spreads down my hill, to my neighbors and those down the road. To those who live in the valley, and in that moment this God I know asks, *Even them?* The perfect point delivered with such precision. That's how it is with that voice. I know who he speaks of. I know why he asks this question so softly, certain, timely.

I consider wrongs done and who did them. Who lives with whom and where they might be, residing down the road from me. In this perfect moment, on this night beneath this moon full of a grace that is larger than I am, I whisper, *Yes, even them*, with all sincerity.

For this moment, on this night, I am who I long to be. And all is well with my soul.

22

Merge with Caution

I've seen the green flash as the sun has set in the Gulf of Mexico. I've seen a blue shooting star so low it dared to burn the outstretched tree. I've seen the end of a rainbow fall in the Atlantic Ocean as surfers paddled to sit beneath the light. I've seen some other things fully supernatural beyond all those afforded to me through nature.

For generations people have looked to the sky, to the rocks, to the water, to the gods they made or the one they discovered, for the answer to appear. We are a people who look for, put our hope in, signs and wonders. Awe holds its special place in our world. Those stars, those winds, those lights. We are the character in the movie, the tempest that stands before the large window and says, "Show me the magic!" and so God casts lightning bolts that stretch across the sky.

Now there is a great distraction. We've seen tricks and sleights of hand. We've seen monuments disappear before our very eyes. We've watched battles in galaxies far, far away. Experienced thrill rides without leaving our chairs. It's all an illusion. How do silent wonders stack up to these? What signs in single colors captivate?

We create in all our great technologies things that materialize before us. And wondrous they are. Beautiful or mesmerizing to behold. Yet they have all issued forth from our hands, our minds, and in our time. Executed in this three-dimensional single, simple world of ours. Those other signs and wonders are from beyond. They originate from a place we don't know. And whether we see them in all actuality or we are seeing something no other naked eye would see makes no never mind. It is the breakthrough of one dimension to another. The communication of a creator with the created. For such a time as this. For some single purpose perhaps that will yet unfold. A message or a confirmation.

Those things I have seen that come from behind the veil are in their own right spectacular, mysterious, wondrous. But then they are gone. The memory of them lingers. Potent at first in a soul-shaking kind of way. Then day by day they fade into a map of where I've been, something that happened as a part of my personal story. The water bill is due again. The baby is sick. I can't find one shoe. The miracle of those signs is a thread in a larger tapestry of my life. I experienced them. I do not live by them. My faith does not rely on them. Nor should it.

What matters regarding seeing signs is how I spend my time in my wakeful, ordinary hours. The condition of my heart as I merge on I-40 traffic. The temperament in my tone when I speak to my mother.

All those stars, flashes, and rainbows I saw because I was looking up. Expectantly. Already in a state of awe and wonder at the splendor that surrounds us. The other things are neither conjured nor conceived. They simply are. Or have been. There is the possibility that I will never have another supernatural moment in my life. But there are the dawn, the dusk, and all the moments in between. Pure and perfect.

23

The God Picture

(A letter to a young granddaughter)

Dear Anna,

The other day I drew a picture for you. It was in response to your asking me what I thought God looked like. That was curious to finally come about because what used to captivate you was the idea of angels. That developed after I had told you a bedtime story about a friend who had a close encounter with an angel and you said, "I have never seen an angel in my life." Like it was the most frustrating thing this side of forever. You were not quite five, and it cracked me up the way you said it. As if everyone you knew or would ever know would go through life seeing angels, but never you.

I suppose if I had created angels I would have given them wings, magnificent ones of iridescent gold. Now that you have me considering this, I'm wondering why we don't have wings. I would very much like wings.

I've saved the pictures that you drew me. Some are from letters that you mailed me and some from our adventures together on summer road trips. In most of them you drew a sun that is smiling. In all of them there is you and me. There *might be a flower or a tree, but no matter what, we are always happy in these pictures, and I treasure them.*

I was going to draw you a picture of God as I know him. First I drew a picture of me and a picture of you. Here is me and here is you. We are happy just because we are together. Then I started to draw God, and I stopped because my paper was too small. God is just that big. And untamable. God defies depiction. Is all encompassing, without end. That's a tough picture to draw. The artist Michelangelo painted God on the Sistine Chapel, and I have been there to see it. It is a beautiful work of art, but still, God is more than that. I just stared at the paper and thought of God. Finally, I thought I could draw a piece of God. See little yellow lights. Those little drops of light are what I think God feels when he looks down and sees you and me. We are God's happy place.

All my other thoughts about God run off the paper.

Love you always, my Anna, from here and beyond,
Zaza

24

The Veil of the Vatican

I have heard of this place called the Vatican all of my life. I knew it was where the pope lived and not much more. Then I knew it was the place where the pope lived and the Sistine Chapel was, which held the work of Michelangelo. As the years ensued, it developed in my mind as more of an amusement park than a holy site. A tourism destination where people would go to check that box. That's how I arrived at the border of the country that is known as the Vatican. I was a tourist in Europe with thirty-six hours in Rome, and seeing the Sistine Chapel was on my list of must-dos. I had forgotten that the Vatican was a country unto itself, and as such one must produce a passport to enter. I was in line at the ticket booth along with nuns from Venezuela and Hasidic rabbis from New York. Out of that group, I felt the most Mickey Mouse of them all. The least devout, the least on pilgrimage. The least expectant, perhaps.

I reach my point in line, the man stamps my passport, and I step through the gate and onto the grounds where the main cathedral sits. There are beautiful buildings and gorgeous fountains. There are people everywhere, and indeed there is that sense of theme park enthusiasm running through the crowd as they chat excitedly and take selfies in lightning-fast rounds. Only I am doing none of these things. I am weeping. I have been crying from the moment my feet crossed over onto the Vatican ground. Everyone else is going on about their visit. But I have been waylaid by a mysterious sense of connection. By some holy mystery, a sense of layers upon layers of prayers. Surprised by the unexpected. Caught off guard.

I walk a little slower, am a little more circumspect and a lot more respectful. The Sistine Chapel is still my focus, but now something else has happened, and, as if a switch has been turned on, my spiritual receptors are firing. I have an odd craving for communion. For hushed prayer. It is the height of European vacation time—August—so hushed prayers are unlikely. The chapel is packed. There are signs telling us that no cell phones and no picture-taking are allowed and that all people should be silent. None of these rules are likely to be followed or are capable of being enforced in August. People chatted, they chattered, they snapped pictures. The guards continuously walked through, warning, No talking, No photos. I am sitting on a bench against the wall, gazing up at God, at the *Erythraean Sibyl* and her message. Surely, here I would receive some message, some confirmation, some amazing spiritual insight. I am closing my eyes and pretending to be there alone. I am planning to return when no one is allowed on vacation in the whole world and I can sit in solitary silence in the chapel of the Sistine. I open my eyes. The images are overwhelmingly beautiful, more beautiful, in fact, than I expected. Grander than all the photos in the world can relate. But the noise of other tourists steals into my visit. I am still searching for that something I sensed when I first arrived.

Then I found it.

It is a small chapel almost hidden away. As if someone must be a seeker to even discover that it was a place. Here there was respect for divinity, the silence and reverence like I had once felt in a cathedral in New York. One much like this, where, once I passed all the tourists, the signs, the guards, I discovered the place where there is an altar, and, before the altar, a small body of people kneeling, whispering their prayers. If they spoke at all, their words were meant for God alone. I knelt among them, my ears not understanding the language of their supplication, but my heart understanding everything.

25

Walkabouts and Riptides

Malcolm Guite—author, chaplain, and musician—relates this reflection as a part of his life journey: As a young man of nineteen, he had been an atheist but found himself moving toward what he defined as a more "open spirituality," but certainly not that of being a Christian. He decided to set out on foot, walking in Ireland. In keeping with his new spiritual sensibilities, he decided not to carry a map, choosing instead in a Zen kind of way to allow the road to lead him. If you had met Malcolm in person, this would be so easy for you to picture. If someone says point to the druid in the room, all fingers would fly in his direction. He is one of the most powerful orators on Christianity I've ever heard.

Upon this walkabout of his, clearing a headland, he came upon this scene:

> I came round a headland at sunset into a beautiful little bay and inlet on the west coast in Donegal, just as the fires were being lit around the headlands for St. John's Eve, and there was drinking and fiddle playing and dancing round the fires that evening. And I asked where I was, and they said Glencolmcille, and I felt a sudden quicken-

ing and sense of connection, as though a memory stirred. And they asked me my name and I said "Malcolm," and they said, "Ah that is why you have come, because he has called you," and I said "who?" and they said "Colm has called you, Malcolm, for this is the place he fought his battle and gathered his disciples and from here he left for the white martyrdom and Scotland." And they told me the story of St. Columba, and the battle he had fought, of his repentance, his self-imposed exile, his journey with twelve disciples from this glen to Scotland where he founded the abbey of Iona from whence Scotland and much of the north of England was converted. "Of course he is calling you here," they said, "for your name in Gaelic means 'servant of Colm,' which is Columba." And as they spoke I remembered at last, right back into my childhood, how I had been told stories about this saint, and how I was named for him, and how my grandmother had published poems about him and sung her lullaby for the infant Columba over me as a child.

Some might call it serendipity or chance. I call it the Holy Spirit. The timing of details dripping in symbolism and historical significance in our lives. Malcolm's poem about this moment is captured in his collection *The Singing Bowl*. What beauty lies in these incredible moments in our lives where all majesty and heavenly hosts seem to orchestrate the divine timing of our footsteps. For people to be there waiting to celebrate our arrival, testifying to us by their presence that we do indeed walk in the path of spiritual significance.

What captivates me most about Malcolm's story, though, is not the circumstances that bring him there at precisely the right moment. It's not even the fact that his grandmother prayed and spoke this story over him as a child, as amazing as that is. It's what he has written about that moment in regard to the Zen philosophy of not carrying a map:

"The map is not the reality! You must utterly and absolutely be in the place you're in, and let that place be what it is and teach what it has to teach without any overlay from your maps and preconceptions."

This is where I am now. Trying to be in the imperfect place of where I am right now. And it is so imperfect in so many ways. This is what I find myself concentrating on. The kind of thing that screams, *I used to be in a higher place.* I have seen supernatural things I may never see again. Surely, I caused this open window to that other world by being a better person at that time in my life. Therefore, to reach those spiritual highs again, reason dictates that I must be better than I am today. Faster, stronger, slimmer. More prayed up, centered, calm in every circumstance. But this is not the advice I'd give you should you come to me asking of things. Concerned about your position or your progress. I would echo the words of Malcolm Guite referring to maintaining a Zen frame of mind.

I could write a numbered list of what I think the picture of my life would look like if I were getting it right. There would be numbers involved. Numbers in my bank account. Numbers on the scale. Numbers of good deeds, thoughtful notes, prayers. I am not sure those are the numbers of God's concern. I feel myself become very pharisaical in my own life. The mirror I keep before me etched upon a scale of my own creation and imagination. Good, not good. Bad, better.

Recently, I had the pleasure of swimming in the warm waters of the Gulf of Mexico on Panama City Beach. My old stomping grounds. I had been wanting to do this for a year, but last time I was down an injury kept me out of the water. It was almost another year before I could make it back during summer weather. This time, I was all in, spending hours upon hours swimming against the current, I rolled and dove with the waves. Sunlight played on the water; a young man wrestled with an oversized pink flamingo float that appeared to be waging a war with him. Children screamed in joy, and lovers held hands. I dove beneath a wave, rose to the surface, and felt the warm sun on my face, the taste of salt on my lips. Salt water heals everything, including broken hearts.

I continued out into the deeper water. I felt a familiar but forgotten sensation. Until it was upon me. As I turned to swim to shore, the water itself pulled me into deeper waters. Edging me farther and farther out by the smallest of degrees, which I knew from being a native was dangerously deceptive. It was the undertow. The tide that pulls you out to sea. The tricky thing is you usually just don't know until it's too late.

I fought fast-rising panic, but only for the slightest of moments. As I struggled to swim back to where I could touch down and walk to some degree between the waves, I remembered you have to swim parallel to the shore until you escape the current, then you can make it to shore. I did this but much farther down the beach. Eventually I walked back on the sand up the beach to my chair. I was drying off when a woman who had told me earlier she was visiting from Arkansas leaned over and asked what the red flag flying high meant.

"Red flag?" For the first time I'd looked at the pole. Indeed, a red flag was flying high. Then I looked back at the water's edge and farther out. It was filled with swimmers. The kind who were already red skinned and sunburned. The kind who had big, blow-up toys and floats and who might not be able to swim very well. The sunny, bright sky looked as if all was easy. "It means you really shouldn't be in the water. It means the currents are strong and can sweep you away." I hadn't checked the flags any more carefully than these visitors determined to have a good time.

I was considering all of this in the ensuing few days. Wanting to be better in so many ways, to get the numbers in my life to line up, fall into alignment. Thinking of that riptide and my trying to get back to the sand. The fear and concern of being pulled farther away from shore.

I began to contemplate: What if God is there on the shore, and all my mistakes and bad habits, my miscalculations, are what's pulling me under and keeping me away from God?

Then a switch flipped and I looked at things from a different perspective. What if God is the rip current? What if the shore is not where I belong? What if my mistakes are not cured or corrected by my furious paddling? What if the answer is to lean back, arms outstretched, eyes cast heavenward, and breathe?

Malcolm's advice wrapped inside his great story is spot-on. Today it is my lesson, speaking to me right in the middle of my mess and my mapless existence. I have considered my struggles to not exactly hide my faith in God but to also not be public, open, or revealing about it But then there is that pulling again. Even as I struggle to reach the familiar shores of my life, to hold on to all the things that so easily beset me, God never lets me go. Deep continues to call to deep. Always. And the riptide of my life continues aligning circumstances so that the words that are my most private, personal experiences in God find their way to the shores of your life.

26

Messengers and Mercury

*W*e all need our messengers. I had Mad Dog Jack when I needed him most. But there have been others, and there still are. They reach out and touch our lives in the strangest, darnedest ways. They appear when we least expect them. A face in a passing car, a stranger's smile on an elevator, a man on the street. Sometimes a knock on the door or a knock in a dream. I've always found one thing interesting about them: they are often very human in nature. And the type of messenger usually depends a lot on the person on the receiving end of things.

Fables and myths always possess a messenger, and often one who controls the bridge between one world and another. This life and the afterlife. The Romans tapped Mercury for this reason, and a grand statue of Mercury sits atop the beautiful Union Station Hotel, which was the original train station back in the day. All those trains coming and going, the sound of them, the sound of the passengers embarking and disembarking. Railroads cornered romance when it came to covering some miles. Nothing is sexier than the rails and the sound of a typewriter. A typewriter on a train in the bar car.

That's the kind of angel I'd like to have show up. One who

traveled by train and wore sunglasses. Or the beer-guzzling, chocolate cookie–smelling angel John Travolta played in the movie *Michael*. Or maybe I'd get lucky and get Holly Hunter's last-chance angel, Earl, of the tobacco-chewing and spitting variety. Holly Hunter spent three years playing the lead in the television show *Saving Grace*. She played Grace Hanadarko, a tough, hard-drinking detective with arms ripped with muscles so tight that on close-ups you could see the blood pump through her veins. She carried one six-pack on her stomach and one in her hand as her character climbed through a lot of darkness trying to live her life. (I fast-forwarded through the sex parts, because there was more than one and I get this creeped-out voyeur feeling, but that's just me.) A pastor's wife told me not too long ago that she absolutely loved *Saving Grace*, but I don't know that her church knew that. Her secret's safe with me, naked butts and all. And that Earl character? Well, if liberties were taken, they were taken very well. Special effects and all. Kudos to the creator of a daring series on faith that featured a few honest-to-God Christians who weren't stereotypical pansies, and to the incredible casting that cornered some well-deserved Emmys.

We need messengers in our lives. Someone to show up and shine some kind of light on the path ahead of us, to say *this way, that way, this way, that way*. It would make it so simple if we knew the right decision to make. Every. Single. Time.

But we don't. And we won't.

Granted, the more time I spend in that silent place of prayer, of listening, the more likely I am to get it right. I wish I could live and breathe and move from that place. Truly, 'tis my desire. In the meantime, I battle-crawl my way through life like everyone else. I just happen to be looking over my shoulder at the mystics of the past, all those saints and sinners who seemed to passionately search for God. Who, when they found a piece of him, clung to that perpetual light and somehow survived. In their own way, they are my messengers, their stories surfacing through history, finding their way to me. The obscure or famous figures stepping from behind the veil of divine mystery.

27

Good Girls Don't Get Naked

I have been raised with certain sensibilities and more rights than wrongs. Taught from an early age to believe in Jesus, to take care of family, and to keep my clothes on. There were other simple lessons to learn. There were two types of girls: good ones and whores. They were easy to distinguish because whores took their clothes off.

I have a photo of my grandmother standing in the middle of a patch of sun-scorched earth. It was taken during a time of drought and dry cotton. She is tall and thin and has the look of a woman whom life has run through hard. Her back is bent and spent from years of picking cotton. Not a cheerful person, not given to whims or fancies, but a strong woman, full of truth and worry. She was a good woman who kept her clothes on.

It was common knowledge that I was one of the favored grandchildren. I think the favor just came from choices I made. I chose to sit at her feet coloring instead of playing outdoors with cousins. To stay by her side in the kitchen as she stirred chocolate into cakes. To rock dreamily in her lap before the fire. I was like Mary at Jesus's feet. Her company was good to keep. And now, all these years since she has been gone, some odd days

I still sense her near me, sense that she is watching me and that she knows. Everything. Including the number of times I have taken off my clothes. In public.

There is a road in Panama City that runs along the bay waters of the Cove. It circles through in a lazy, residential way, shaded with old oaks dripping with moss, with magnolias and tall pines. A sleepy, salty place where families settle and raise their kids the right way. And it is here, in a hidden cove, that I first got naked.

It was at the urging of that new best friend from seventh grade. I slept over one night, and we walked the neighborhood in a meandering, seventh-grade way. Nothing but Saturday-afternoon sunshine and time. We followed a road that dodged to the left, where the houses stopped and the wildness of old Florida remained. A road that ended in dirt and sand and low palms and scrub pines. On the other side of this undeveloped land lay a cove of water inland from the bay.

"Let's get naked," Cathy said, kicking off her sandals.

"What?" I was a shy girl. Careful. Getting naked in broad daylight with someone I'd only known a few weeks didn't seem like a Momma-approved idea.

"Let's go skinny-dipping."

I looked at her.

"Naked," she said, as if I was a bit slow. "Let's swim naked."

It was nowhere near sundown. There was no cover of darkness to hide my sin.

"We'll get caught," I said, stalling.

"Who's going to catch us?"

I looked around. A bomber squad of low-flying pelicans was the only witness.

The hidden shores of the Cove lagoon would one day be developed and would showcase the expensive houses of charming people. Houses where years and years later I would gather at literary dinners and talk writing with best-selling authors. But back then, it was still wild.

Cathy unzipped her jeans, slid right out of them. I stayed put, weighing the war within me. Do right. Do wrong. Then her T-shirt flew up, and off, and she didn't stop there. Her bra quickly followed, then her underwear.

She was "naked as a jaybird," as my aunt Leaner would say. My granny would have just pursed her lips and looked the other way in order not to cast her eyes on my doing wrong. Every whore had a beginning. I was pretty certain I didn't want to be a whore.

Cathy swam backward, flipped over, dived back into the blue water. I watched, envious now of her obvious lack of burden. She swam a few guiltless strokes farther out and yelled back, "C'mon!"

Do right? Do wrong? Hesitantly, I took off my shirt, looked around, quickly unzipped my jeans. I pulled off all my clothes as if I were on fire.

I swam, dived, flipped, and felt the sun on my chest, thinking surely a feeling that good just couldn't be bad. There was all this warm water and the sun and wind and a deliciousness that lulled me into an embryonic state. One I didn't remember from that terrifying birth when I was jerked from the womb.

Still there was an underlying sense that I was somehow being bad. That I had one wet foot over the county line to Hookerville.

Cathy and I never swam naked again. We tried once, but when we arrived there were boys on bikes riding the dirt road and kicking up sand, so it wasn't the same. But that secret Saturday baptized us into becoming best friends for many lazy summers yet to come.

I did not become a whore, but where naked has been, naked will come again.

28

Sometimes Good Girls Get Naked

*T*here's a road in north Florida known as 30A. It turns off of Highway 98 and runs along the beach for sixteen miles. Now it has become famous for so many things—Seaside, Rosemary Beach, Sundog Books, Bud and Alley's Restaurant, Grayton Beach, Red Roof Bar, Criolla's, Blue Mountain Beach. But on this night when I am fifteen, the beaches of north Florida have real sand dunes that curve around the warm Gulf Coast waters like white treasure. This was before the huge spring break clubs, before the condos that stripped the beach and blocked the view.

At fifteen I was still a good girl. I waited tables in the summer and went to school in the fall. I did my homework, did my chores, made good grades, made my curfews. It was my birthday, and to celebrate I piled into a van with friends and we headed toward the beach and 30A. We were a motley group, clinging to the fringe of an old neighborhood that was getting older. We were kids of pastors and sergeants, mill workers and salesmen. It was a time of Tolkien, of summers filled with lazy beaching, of AM radio. A time of Friday-night concerts and Simon & Garfunkel. We were all in love with the "we" of us.

We had loaded down the van with coolers, Cokes, chips, and blankets, and, in honor of my birthday, chocolate brownies.

We parked the van on the side of the deserted road and carried our stuff high to keep it dry, wading through the lagoon waters to get to the other side. We built a bonfire and told stories under a night sky raging with stars.

Then suddenly, with little discussion, we were peeling off our clothes and we were laughing, running, diving into moonlit waves lazily rolling up on white sands. And of all the nights, phosphorescence filled the water so that as we swam we were moving light like a reflection of those stars above us. Some of us have died now. By accident, by illness, by suicide. I guess the rest of us are simply growing older, until we are all gone. But on that night, on my birthday, we were so young we were immortal.

29

Running Naked Is Good for You

*T*here is a road that runs due south from north Florida to south Florida. It takes you through groves laden with oranges to a place filled with money where the homes of the wealthy are cradled by their ocean view. It is a different country, where the winds turn warmer and the palms grow five stories high.

My only bona fide vacation of my life as a kid was to Rock City in the third grade with Momma and Daddy. And Rock City has always held a special magic in my heart. A place we took the Adorables a few years ago and they caught it, loved it, too.

But there was one other surprise. A vacation that came out of left field. Mom surprised me and Cousin Deb and her mother, my aunt Margie, with a week in West Palm. Alone, Deb and I were pretty good girls. Even at seventeen, we managed to steer clear of trouble. But together we were notorious. We were trouble. And a litany of stories and shenanigans will always follow us through this life.

At fifteen, we stole our cousin Brenda's convertible in the small town of Altha, Florida, down by the river. She ran after us on foot until we were out of sight, driving the country back roads just for the thrill, the top down, laughing all the way.

We jumped from high trees into raging waters and almost drowned. We got lost and found. We sneaked out and partied all night and didn't get caught until Daddy found us sneaking in at sunrise. He promptly delivered us to my mother the queen, who would pass out a verdict and mete justice. We were to be separated for the rest of our lives.

Two years later, we weren't running the roads of our neighborhood but were in West Palm Beach, Florida, where the palms grew taller than we had ever seen. We were on a real vacation for the first time, not just a drive to visit all our Southern relatives. A vacation made sweeter by the fact that it was February, and our friends back home were in school. Somehow my mother had managed to convince the school to let us go for seven school days. We were giddy, running on a jailbreak high.

The family checked into a seven-story Holiday Inn with an ocean view, where we would eat seafood and laze our days away by the pool, turning a glorious winter brown that we would carry back to school to the envy of beach-loving friends. West Palm Beach was rich, foreign. It was our Paris. On one particular night in this rich, south Florida town on an eight-lane landscaped boulevard that ran between the hotel and the water, along a boulevard filled with rich people driving rich cars, on the hotel grounds below our room, in a grove of blooming azaleas, we shucked off all our clothes.

"So here's the plan," Deb said.

My cousin Deb was a God-blessed, natural-born athlete. She had spent summers riding me on the handlebars of a bike. She had walked five hundred steps on her hands every day in the summer, just for something to do. She could dive, swim, run, jump, and whip a man at tennis. And now she was telling me, her bookworm, best-friend, buddy-cousin, to take off my clothes and run for the bushes. I was not beyond a dare. I don't look competitive, but occasionally something rises up in me that will surprise even me. This was one of those times.

I stripped down to nothing and clutched my clothes in my hand. Bare naked, and this time, there was no warm water waiting to embrace me in a skinny-dipping moment, just the sound of the traffic next to us, those palms slapping in the wind high above as we both yelled, "One, two, three, go!"

As I took off, it dawned on me that I was naked. In public. On an eight-lane boulevard. I can't say shame overcame me, because it wasn't shame. It was true modesty. Modesty is hard to pull off when you are running naked. It is quickly replaced by a great sense of panic.

In the midst of this moment, what surpassed the sound of the cars passing, the palm trees slapping, the distant waves, my heartbeat, and the occasional horn was the sound of my cousin, the Olympian athlete, laughing so hard she couldn't run. I realized that what was causing her such naked mirth was the sight of my rear end streaking hard as you please across that wide expanse of manicured green. I was shooting for a group of azaleas that appeared to be a football-field length away. She was laughing so hard she had forgotten she was naked. She was doubled over somewhere behind me. I made it to the bushes and was clothed again before she could catch up to me.

Being bad with a relative seems like less of a sin, as if we had taken naked and divided it by two. I was guilty at half-weight, relieved at the feel of my clothes on my back, and was laughing too hard to worry about calculating degrees of sin.

30

Naked Is Natural

Once upon a time, in a life before this life I now live, there was an island and on it a solitary house that faced out toward the waves. A place of luck and lore. A place of story. Then it got to become a part of mine. Even if just for a short time.

We reached Shell Island by boat and were dropped off in the breaking waves, just off the beach before the house. My sons were still boys. There was just us and the island and one lone, perfectly primitive house.

Pelicans flew in low every day, skimming the water. We counted twenty-seven once, the largest squadron we saw, the same as my age at the time. A pelican for every year.

For days we played cards and checkers. We watched thunderheads roll in and lightning streak across the water. We wandered the sand searching for shells. Bones of fish. Bottles washed ashore. We collected these treasures. We lived without power, lighting candles to eat dinner. The sun rose and we woke. The sun slept and we rested. We became naturally human.

After days, we washed our naked bodies in the gulf to save our drinking water. I stood at a small distance from the boys—washing quickly, black clouds on the horizon, a mighty storm brewing and headed in fast. They were little boys still, but not babies. Yet there I was, naked, if only for minutes. And right at that moment, this one naked moment, a photo was taken.

I didn't realize it until after the film was developed, and then there it was, proof that I was—naked. From a distance, mind you. A pretty good distance. It would be so easy to discard. It's not digital. Not Facebooked. An old photo, now yellowed with time. I've started to throw it away a dozen times, but I cannot. I always put it back and hide it behind photographs of other photographs and keep it hidden there. Hidden—and protected. This wild photo on an island, storm clouds circling, gulf waves lapping at our bodies.

I save it because we are all as innocent and as young as we will ever be beyond that moment. In this photograph you can see that innocence. It surfaces and remains so many years later. From a distance, as Bette Midler once sang, God is watching us from a distance. I think he smiled.

31

Naked Came I

*T*here's a stretch of road in the American West where you could wander waterless for days. Wander until the sun burned the clothes from your body, till you were nothing but white bone. Depending on your direction, this road delivers you to swampy air and salt waters, or to high deserts full of sky, a place of a different kind of wonder where you can see the shadows of clouds sailing across the landscape. There is an aloneness in this place that calls to you. It called to me once and found me. It calls to me still.

New Mexico gives me something no other place can. Orange neon sunsets to stop a clock. The air full of places I haven't been. Flat rocks, and cold streams, and the gorge that stunned me silent when I first laid eyes on it. The rawness of the earth split open, exposing ancient mysteries. And then, of course, there is the light.

It takes twenty-three hours and seventeen minutes to drive from Panama City to Taos. A little over twenty-four if you stop for gas and coffee. I hit Tucumcari at midnight, the smell of sage on the air. There's more room in this country than you can fathom. I pull the top off the thermos filled up at the last truck stop on I-40. It's one o'clock as I take a right turn, head up State Road 84.

I'm twenty-one hours in, and if I manage to hang on for a few more hours, if I can just stay awake and not fall asleep at the wheel, I'll be there, grab our things, load the car. I've used the miles to clear the clutter from my mind.

The lightning intensifies, the dark sky now spitting fire. The horizon is cluttered with clouds. Lightning rips on the horizon across that blackness, illuminating nothing but the flat-top mesas stretching out for miles and miles—and me.

There are many kinds of alone, but there is only one that is the alone of driving through the high desert at two a.m. Fighting the beast of sleep, I unbutton my shirt, shift hands on the wheel, shuck my clothes—one arm, one shoulder at a time—until I am bare chested driving into the storm. I roll the windows down, stick my arm out into the electric air.

In just my jeans and boots I ride alone on this planet riddled with light and dark, full of shifting shadows. I am the first life and the last life. I am Eve in the wilderness of God's creation. My foot on the pedal, pushing to dawn, to deliverance, to destiny.

And I am not ashamed.

32

Dog and Cat Take a Ride

*I*t appeared, for all practical purposes, that hell was breaking loose. Or that angels of destruction and all those seals and the apocalypse might be a real thing, and that it might be happening. There seemed to be nowhere in the world that was safe, no corner of the globe or country that was not at risk of calamity. Tornadoes and cave-ins, earthquakes and floods, blizzards and raging storms that would neither weaken nor seem to end. As a strange coincidence, perhaps, Steve Carell stars in a new movie release *Evan Almighty*, a comic re-creation of the story of Noah building an ark—complete with beard and boards, animals and disbelieving neighbors. A flood shows up, so all is not without need and merit. As the action continues to take place offscreen, one can only assume that they all live happily ever after.

But we weren't quite at the ever-after stage; it was just looking a whole lot like ever-after might be coming sooner than we expected. Fires rage, storms grow, people begin to shake a little in their boots, watching the sky for signs of impending doom. Thinking that they really ought to tackle that final Harry Potter book before the end of everything. Fires in California took four hundred thousand acres; an earthquake in Peru claimed five hundred lives; there were tropical storms in

Pakistan. Tornadoes in Kansas eradicated an entire town. All of it was child's play when a storm hit Bangladesh and took five thousand with one sweep. Being a little nervous was in order. But one person seemed unmoved by all the shaking going on.

Steve Jobs moved through the year with a confident, gangly gait and right up onto the stage to reveal the first iPhone. Snap, pop, crackle—history is made. And all the Apple consumers go *Awww*.

In the middle of this melee, an author buddy and I went on a book tour together. If I knew how to draw cartoons or comics, I would sketch the entire trip, because it perfectly illustrated the absolute absurdity of life, the comic turns, the poignant moments. We were crisscrossing states like book bandits hitting one store and then another. We were a whirlwind of words and stories. And prayers.

I have never been more like someone in every way—and at the same time, completely different—in my life. I don't think it would be possible for it to happen again. The odds are too wild. I've never believed the same thing or worshipped the same God, but in a completely different way. We are two sides of one coin. But it stands to me as an example that coins always have two sides. The relationship that has grown and deepened over the years reminds me to remember to be myself and to realize that just because other people aren't like me, it doesn't mean they're wrong. Or that I'm right. It means we are certainly all part of an eternal story and that if we relax along the way a little, sometimes we are in for a wild ride.

If I were a fairy-tale writer, this is the way it would begin: Once upon a time, a dog and a cat went on a ride. They drove far and wide over the countryside to read to people and tell some stories. Along the way they had great adventures and escaped great perils. They lost almost everything they had, time and time again. They found almost everything they lost, time and time again. At the end of the long, long journey they went back home to their families and their lives. But they never forgot their adventures because they had told layers of stories and they knew this was just the beginning.

Or some such thing. The fact was, Shellie Rushing Tomlinson and I knew each other because we had met where half the writers I know met, and that's at Kathy Murphy's Pulpwood Queens Girlfriend Weekend. It's a wild time in a Texas town as the world at large meets and talks to celebrate authors and the written word and to have a little fun. Primarily a women's event (a few straggling husbands show up each year and a few attending writers are male), the whole weekend is pink, complete with feathers and tiaras, a themed costume party, an authors' dinner where the authors serve the dinner and do the dishes (imagine looking up to see Pat Conroy pouring your tea), and many panels and authority presentations. It is truly an original and one-of-a-kind experience.

The year I met Shellie, I walked into that auditorium to see her in the back with her laptop set up and working on something. I sat down and opened up my laptop. I had work to do on an upcoming radio program and was considering some recording possibilities. Turns out she was too, as she has a radio program. And that's how it began. There was also the fact that other authors were chatting and having fun and relaxing as we sat there having fun and chatting and desperately working to get one more thing done. Then we started swapping stories.

That was probably the thing that cinched things right there. So at some point in the coming year, we talked about doing a self-created book tour on our own—together. One we put up the bucks for and did on a shoestring. No, make that a wing and a prayer—and that became the official title of the tour. What ensued was the wild adventure of story tales. We took the show on the road. Shellie drove up from Louisiana and spent one night with me. We hopped in my Jeep, which was now part of our official logo for the tour, thanks to her creative son-in-law, and officially kicked off the tour with an authors' lunch at the Loveless Cafe. From there we had planned to hit the Natchez Trace, which is one of the greatest little road-trip beauties, and drive straight down to one of our favorite bookstores, Reed's Gum Tree Bookstore in Tupelo, Mississippi, owned by the renowned and knightly Mr. Jack Reed, Sr.

We lunched, we took photos, we said our good-byes to the other authors, and we took a few photos for our on-the-road blog. At this point, we had garnered official sponsors, like the hot sauce company that gave us merchandise to give away to readers along every stop. We snap our pictures and go to get in the Jeep—only I can't find my keys. As we are looking for my keys, Shellie lays down her new and highly important Nikon camera with its official neck strap to look for said keys. When we find the keys and return to our car, we realize she has lost her camera. As we look for her camera, I lose my cell phone and have to go back into the Loveless for the third time, asking if they have found our missing items. In the space of seven minutes. They began to look at me like I was on drugs. I needed to try to explain that I wasn't on drugs but there was a strong possibility that maybe I should be. A customer found Shellie's camera and delivered it safely to us, and, with said keys and, eventually, two phones, we got in the Jeep, which was packed to the gills with clothing and laptops and radio electronics, as we were determined to post shows and MP3s and interviews and photos and blog all along the way. God bless our overachieving little hearts.

We sat in the Jeep with the keys, the camera, the cell phones, and took a deep breath. We hadn't driven two feet and we were off schedule already. It was the first time both of us became aware that the other person on this little tour had a problem, the same problem: losing things while they were still in our hands. Shellie looked at me and said, "I didn't know you had this problem too; I had hoped one of us would be the kind of person who kept up with things, and I knew it wasn't me."

"Nope," I told her, "me neither. This doesn't bode well for the rest of the journey."

She agreed: "No, it does not." Then she posted a picture of us on Facebook under the Loveless sign as I drove out of the parking lot and onto the Trace. That was the ceremonious beginning of a twenty-one-city, fourteen-day tour. No, that's not quite possible, but we did it anyway, passing out presents along the way. We stayed with author friends and book readers and occasionally in a bona fide hotel. We blogged, posted, photo'd, Twittered, and radio'd all along the way. We interviewed bookstore owners at every stop and took pictures of their stores. From the outside looking in, it appeared to be a whole lot of fun. And it was, but it was also a whole lot of work to get to that point and to keep going. We tried not to make it look like work. I think we did a pretty good job of that.

Along the way, from city to city, we had plenty of time to swap stories, and we had them stacked and racked and piled up. Shellie couldn't tell a story that wouldn't remind me of one I needed to tell her, and vice versa. We began to have to take notes to get back around to them. The one about Uncle Dan, the story of Celia, the one about my cousin getting a suntan, and on and on. There is no end to how much we both love a good story. I have a good feeling that God does too, what with Jesus teaching in parables and all that stuff.

We also talked a little bit about faith. Just a little. And to tell the truth, not a whole lot, because it became apparent that we both had a deep and abiding faith and that we had another thing in common: we didn't preach it so much as live it. It wasn't something either of us put in a back pocket to whip out at the earliest convenience—it just was. When you room up close with someone and you travel with them, you learn some things. Like when I first reach my next destination, a hotel room, a friend's bedroom, a bedroll somewhere, I like to kneel down for a moment and just give thanks for making it that much farther along the journey. For safe travels. Shellie would wake up and hit her knees, a good-morning kind of prayer while I stumbled for the coffeepot.

All those miles on the road clocked over two thousand, all told. Shellie loved her husband. Ditto. Shellie loved her kids. Ditto. Her mama and daddy, her grands, and so on, and ditto, ditto, ditto. We are each plugged up with family love. A little possessive of them, a little "drop it all like it's on fire and rush to them" kind of thing. We are both likely to try to juggle grandbabies and deadlines all at the same time.

But there were differences, such as:

Shellie listened to praise and worship music that she wanted to share with me as I drove with earphones in. She assured me that it was very beautiful and inspiring and she really wanted me to hear it. I took out my earphones and listened. Then she said, "Just one more," and I listened. It was all those things she said it was.

And when I said, "I have to put my earphones back in now so I can listen to Dire Straits sing 'Brothers in Arms' again because for some strange reason it really ministers to me," she said okay.

And there were times such as:

The night we had wrapped up a reading event in Chattanooga and were downtown late at night, walking back to the Jeep, pulling our cases behind us full of recording equipment, when a man stepped out of the shadows and said something like, "Ah, look at you two beautiful ladies." We said something like, "Uh-huh," and kept walking. He followed.

"Listen here, I'll help you, let me help you."

"Nope, we got it, thanks anyway."

"Well let me ask you, can you help a brother out? Just down on my luck, don't you know, and..." And so it continued all the way around the dark corner, down another street, and to the Jeep as we began loading equipment. Now, I can't tell you if we handed him any money or passed him protein bars from the car. But this is what I do remember: suddenly, and I mean suddenly, the man's voice changed. His posture changed. Green fire shot out of his eyeballs and he raised a finger and said, "You need to *slow* down!" Shellie and I stopped what we were doing on opposite sides of the Jeep and looked at him.

"Do you hear what I'm saying? I said you need to *slow* down!" He may have said this three more times in roughly the same way with the same emphasis.

Shellie and I both said, "Okay, thanks, we will," and then we got into the Jeep. I cranked it and drove off down the street. We were both quiet for a little bit, then Shellie said carefully, in consideration of the fact that this was one of our earlier stops along the tour and we still didn't know each other all that well—certainly not as well as we would ten more days down the road—"Um, River, I don't know exactly how you hear from God, but I think that man was giving us a message." I can still hear the gentleness in her voice, which makes me smile thinking about it. The way she was laying out her hearing-from-God case.

"I know that man was all pretty-ladies and help-a-brother-out, but then his voice changed and..."

"Yep, that was God, all right," I told her. "No question about it in my book. What I heard was we needed to slow down under no uncertain terms." Which I think might have given her some relief. I made up the part about the green light out of the eyes, but that would just be a cool special effect. The voice, however, did change, as did the stance, and everything. The man went from all jive and shuffle to the power of a prophet.

The fact is, the next morning we had to drive through the Blue Ridge Mountains on back roads, not interstates. It was raining all day long, and we crept along places where the right tires were ever-so-close to the edge of nothing, without guard rails. There was up and there was down, and there seemed to be no in-between. We encountered not one but two major rock slides, which meant we had to be rerouted, which meant we were not minutes but hours late for our next signing. It was all a great setup to try desperately to speed along on those winding switchbacks, to try to make up time through the rain, through the mud and rocks and low visibility. Only we didn't do what would have come naturally to both of us. There was a powerful echo from the night before still ringing in our ears. And while his eyes really didn't shoot out those sparks, they almost could have by the look in them. It was a very aware look, a look full of warning. And, as different as we are, we both got it. We arrived so late we had to make a return stop to the store the next day, but we arrived. Because we heard.

Shellie said near the end of our tour full of fun and hijinks, with many a day seeming like something close to Lucy and Ethel setting out on the road together, that she had finally figured it out. She was like a dog rushing into the room, tail wagging, smiling, wanting to play, wanting to be petted. I was like a cat, walking silently through the room until I could get to a good window seat and sit down and look out and be undisturbed. Not that I wouldn't come around eventually to purr and play for petting, but it would be in due time, which is always after looking-out-the-window time. She nailed it.

And there are other differences. For instance, if you were a reader who came to an event and met us on book tour and told us you had been having a problem with someone coming along every single year and picking all the figs off your fig tree, and how sad and mad that made you, and that you were thinking about painting a sign with the commandment THOU SHALT NOT STEAL and nailing it to the tree, and you wanted to know what did we think about that or what should you do, this is the way I imagine it going down: Shellie would offer to pray for you. She would pray for your figs and your harvest and your protection. She would pray that angels guard that tree and that you be allowed to eat those figs and make preserves for your family. She wouldn't even wait—she would do it right there before we left. She's so precious that way.

My advice?

I'd tell you to go to the closest grocery store and get you a chicken and some pigs' feet and pork ribs. Then to go home and boil that chicken till the meat slides off the bones and make a big pot of dumplings. To cook those pork ribs, however, you want to cook a mess of greens and some corn bread while you are at it, and then have the family over to eat, but you be the one to pick up the dishes. Then take that chicken and pull it apart so you have a lot of little bones. Take the pork bones and the chicken bones and bleach them till they are white and will not attract wild dogs. Tie little threads to them and hang them on that fig tree. If you've got a piece of colored glass or bottle, hang that too. If you are going to put up a sign of any kind, make it something in Latin. Work the word *muerte* in there. That's important. Let them look that one up.

Because here is the thing:

You are in the South, and whoever has been eating those figs is from the South, and they were raised with those Ten Commandments sure as I'm sitting here typing these words. They already know they shouldn't steal them; they just don't care. So you go on and do what I said, because Scriptures people are used to this. You need to catch 'em by surprise. Make 'em a little bit uncertain. Even if they think it's just a trick, they are going to have a hard time reaching past those bones to pick that fig. I promise you.

Since those miles, we've been in Texas again a few times and had numerous conversations on the phone. One of those conversations was about how we are the same and how we are completely different. How we approach God in different ways and would most likely have a different opinion about a whole lot of religious points of view and cultural hot buttons. I just have to say, "Shellie, how come... Have you ever wondered..." And I never get the entire thought out of my mouth before she says, "I know, I know." The differences abound. The similarities are strange. And somewhere in the middle of all that, there is this meeting in the middle that is right, possibly closer to the truth than either of us knows.

Now when I am worried about one of my children, or a grandchild, when my deadlines have me up against the wall, do you think I reach for a chicken bone? No, I do not. I talk to God. And I call Shellie.

33

The Zombie Truth

I tell my doctor that I hate being on thyroid medicine—
or, more precisely, that I hate that I need to take thyroid
medicine—because if the zombie apocalypse comes, I will not
be able to get my thyroid pills and that will make me slug-
gish and slow and easy for the zombies to get so they can eat
my brains. She gives me an odd look, tells me that I probably
have plenty of other things to worry about besides the zombie apocalypse, and maybe we should concentrate on those
things.

I think, *Sure, you have all those samples stashed. What are you
worried about?*

Zombies. I don't know when they became so popular and
maybe they are already on the way out and something new
will have to take their place, but for a while now they have
been one hot ticket. There are even zombie weddings you can
YouTube, and they are pretty creative. Mates have written their
own vows, even pledging to stand and fight the zombies until
the end—together.

Y2K was a kind of zombie thing, although people weren't
afraid of their brains getting eaten, just of being unplugged

from every technical thing in the world, having no power, no communication, no infrastructure. There has been concern about how society would handle this, since folks are not used to being on their own. No groceries and all that.

During the rumors and the Y2K threats, people were buying beans. I was buying books and settling in for a long season of some good reading. This was my shot at being offline for a while. A little downtime to catch up on my reading, say, to read all the classics, and then we'd pick back up where we left off. But now Y2K seems so yesterday, and now it's zombies that loom on the horizon.

Did you see that movie with Will Smith where he has a German shepherd? That's all he has left in this world, and he's trying to find a zombie cure. That's a scary one. It's a really lonely, scary one. In *World War Z* with Brad Pitt, there are lots of people fighting zombies together, so it's not the same. It doesn't have that alone-in-all-the-world feeling. Having seen both, fighting zombies with your friends is what I recommend.

When I was five and went to the frozen-exile tundra, I had a dream—no, not a dream. It was a nightmare. And in this nightmare, one by one, the entire world began to turn into "the others." I could say zombies, but there was no brain-eating. It was more like an invasion of the body snatchers. One by one, everyone turned into something else until the whole world was gone and it was down to only me and my grandmother. Then they got her too. I stood in the street, watching her look at me out of a curtained window. Then she dropped the curtain, and I was left in the street, five years old and all alone in this entire world. Then I woke up. Charming, huh? Not a dream one easily forgets. I'm past fifty now (and I don't even know how that happened), and it's still visually ingrained in my mind.

But, unlike in my dream, I believe that, should the earth survive all the flying rocks and space trash, if humanity survives our insanity, there will be a band of good guys who will prevail and begin again. In peace. At least in the beginning. Like in the dark and perfect work *The Road*, by Cormac McCarthy.

"We're still the good guys, right, Dad? And we'll always be the good guys." That one voice, that one kid. In the middle of so much death and destruction, that horrible little thing we call *hope* continues.

Rivers: A Novel, by Michael Farris Smith, is another beautifully written example of a narrative that shows the dark side of the end and the hope of a new beginning. I'm drawn to these works for this reason. I want to see that the good in us survives against all odds. In the middle of evils that are so horrific that they are unspeakable, I still believe in the good that is the true human heart.

This surge of dystopian literature is a little frightening in its possibilities. Sometimes fiction precedes the possible. Space travel, for instance, as with H. G. Wells and his classic *The Time Machine*. Except to have dystopia, you have to have bad. Really, really bad. Stephen King did it early, in *The Stand*, maybe the first work I'd ever read along those lines, exploring the theme of the end of time, the showdown between good and evil. Some books don't include the actual battle in supernatural terms, but King's alludes to it. Others are concrete, cut-and-dried, like Cormac's *The Road*. It's man against the environment that's left. Man against man. Woman against child. It's a bloody mess is what it is.

Author Ronlyn Domingue wrote *The Mapmaker's War*, a work of fiction that ultimately points to a more evolved, enlightened society beyond the bands of war and prejudice. We had a long conversation during an interview about the serious possibility that society creates its own reality. About how, if we keep planning and preparing for an apocalypse, it will surely come, and that perhaps we could reset our minds to better things. We could envision a future that prospers in peace and kindness, one where we use our technologies in the right ways to help ease the burden of human suffering. Where we simply and truly agree, yes, to get along. She has a valid point.

As a Man Thinketh, by James Allen, was a work pretty much dedicated to this concept. When it came out, I think it might have gained a lot of criticism in some camps, including the Christian one, for appearing to be something that promoted mind power over divine power. When you are certain what you believe in, you can read a lot of things from different world views and cultivate the good from them. If the thoughts of a man or woman affect their reality I wish my family—all the generations that came before me, what I refer to as the tribe of Eyore—would have grasped the concept of positive thinking. Boil, boil, toil, and trouble was on the minds of a lot of my family members. And that's what came to pass in their lives. In spite of their faith many clung to the dark side of the cloud, not the silver lining. But, in spite of this fact about them, Allen's idea that "circumstance does not make the man, it reveals him to himself" was true. We discovered ourselves in the flames of fire, the obstacles we were faced with and overcame. And I like to believe that in those circumstances we were revealed as good people.

For instance, sometimes you meet people you don't like. Or who don't like you. And it's just that way. I don't know why, but something about either our genetics or our upbringing gives us preset buttons to be more drawn to certain types of people and to run the other way when we see other types of people coming. This is what I do in those situations: even if someone doesn't like me or irritates me in some small way, I imagine if there were a sudden catastrophe, if we were all stranded on the moon from an intergalactic train wreck, what good they'd be. How I'd survive with them. Usually, no matter what our differences, I see them coming up to bat in full swing. I see them bringing what they have to the table for our survival, and it's always something that benefits the rest of us. And it helps me see them in the light of their potential, no matter what they think of me.

When Nathan Englander was interviewed by Terry Gross on NPR's *Fresh Air*, he talked about how the Holocaust was so removed from his family in terms of time and life circumstance, but, at the same time, it was ever present in the household. This knowledge, this awareness, was always in their lives. He told a story about a game he and his sister played when they were younger. When someone came to visit or their parents met someone new, they watched them to figure out if that person would hide them or turn them in.

When a particular couple first came to visit, his sister observed them for a while. "He would hide us," his sister said of one couple, "but she would turn us in."

It's a heartbreaking thought, that one. And it's such a bizarre, quick way to reach some kind of truth about a person.

I hope I'd be one to hide people, but it's a tough place to imagine, what you would be when your back's against the wall. And it's one thing for it to be your back, but when your decision affects your entire family and all your children, the scary stakes get higher.

Maybe we're not supposed to know the truth about ourselves until that moment; we're just supposed to hope and pray that it never comes.

A woman I met the other night at a party talked of being Jewish, and somehow the conversation rolled around to this between tequila tastings, this thing about hiding or not hiding. She said not only would she not hide people, but she'd be saying, "What, are you kidding? I'm Italian." She said it with a Brooklyn accent and Italian lilt. So, over cocktails and tequila, the subject of apocalypse, of holocaust, arises. Perhaps these days it's ever present and it's meant to be. Our taking stock of the now, this present moment. Living fully in the lives that we've been given. Chuck Norris wrote a little book years ago titled *The Secret Power Within* where he talks about Zen and discipline and his life story. It's a fine little book and has a lot of short good points in it, but one story that stands out for me most is one where he went to visit a terminally ill little boy in a hospital who told him, "Yesterday, I had tomorrow." I think the kid was seven, and these are words he uttered.

So I'm back to the zombies and thinking about society crashing in around us and what we need to stockpile in case that happens. I'm thinking toilet paper and tampons, because I'm thinking of the women.

Then I go back to my mental list, but now I keep it to myself. It includes composition books, the old ones with the hard covers and lines, and early readers, and lots of pens and pencils. Because should there be an end of days, there should also be a new beginning, and there must be story. There must be children who learn to read and write and carry on.

You might wonder where God is in the midst of all this "maybe," in all this history and this possible despair. I guess he is in the same place he has always been, allowing us to make monumental decisions that change the course of history. Allowing us to possess brave, small acts of human kindness at great risk. Realizing that in the biggest picture, the frame of things, there is no end.

But in the meantime, I need to relax and realize that telling stories is part of being human; it's integrated into all of us and it runs through and through. And whether it comes down to movie images of the wild children in the *Mad Max* fables, or Tom Hanks around that fire in *Cloud Atlas*, there will be stories to be told.

Because we must always say what it was to continue.

34

Lucy Boards a Train

It's one of those early fall mornings. The kind that makes Americans think of pumpkins and pie. Of Thanksgiving bounty and blessings and tables surrounded by the faces of those we love.

This morning I curl in front of the heater with Annie Dillard's *Pilgrim at Tinker Creek* and Scott Cairns's *Short Trip to the Edge*, also about his pilgrimage. These particular pilgrims make for good company. They are warm and full of genuine humor, but they also possess a deep longing for the person we call God. I can imagine walking along a path with them, whether on the rocky shores of Greece or through the long, dark woods, and being so wordlessly aware of the Divine Presence that we hardly speak at all. And, just as easily, I could imagine sitting in a pub with them on some cold and windy night in a town on the sea and drinking, laughing, and swapping stories. They would be about real people and places. They would be about art and truth. And all of it would be about God. So, yes, Dillard and Cairns are such good company this morning, when I have this book on my mind. I am longing to say so much and fearing that I will never, ever, get it down right. That no matter how hard I try, I will leave something just there, in that ridge, unseen, unheard, unfelt. That I will either not explain myself correctly or I'll overexplain to the point of no return.

Scott writes of meeting a British pilgrim, a scholar who is in the midst of writing about the Lord's Prayer, something called *theosis*, and other spiritual matters. I knew the word *thesis* but I've forgotten it, so I decide I have to look it up and that I need to be quiet and be still and just be, be, be in God's circle. Just hang out with Jesus. Just focus on moving in that river that is the Holy Spirit, a continual wheel of inspiration.

I glance out the window at the sunshine of the morning and the colored, dancing autumn leaves. Dancing, clinging, falling, flying. And I wonder, *What am I doing inside?* I should be standing in the middle of the woods. Walking along my creek like Annie Dillard did hers. Finding my way over the rocks as Scott did for days across the Greek terrain. I should be just there, walking and talking with this being I believe in with all my heart. That I actually trust on my better days, in my better moments.

Then I think about the colored leaves again and how Thanksgiving is coming. About how we used to have Thanksgiving dinner at my grandmother's every year with aunts and uncles and mommies and daddies and cousins and some more cousins and some cousins twice removed. (I have never figured that one out, but I know it's so.)

Then Grandmother became older and moved in with us, and the dinners were moved to our house, and my mother took over the tradition of brothers and sisters and the whole brood gathering around the table. I'm thinking I should host Thanksgiving here. Take on the tribe and the dirty dishes. Which means I need to clean, and maybe I should decorate.

Which leads me to looking up ways to hide the uglies that exist here and there in my house, projects that just likely will not be finished in time for Thanksgiving dinner. So I grab my phone and google *Thanksgiving decorations,* hit Pinterest for a few ideas.

Think "Cue the deer" from Chevy Chase's movie *Funny Farm.* Yes, it's time to cue the deer for the holidays. Then I see that Polyvore has a few messages on the app. I click there and begin looking at fall-themed kinds of things. Then, the next thing you know, I'm looking at leather handbags and find a beauty from Italy for five hundred and something that is exactly what I've been looking for. Now if I can only find that same bag for twenty dollars. Well, maybe if I put in a search for leather handbags from Italy under twenty-five on eBay, something will turn up....

And I'm off. Nothing is done. Nothing is written. I think I might possess a real case of attention deficit disorder. As a matter of fact, I know I do, but so do a lot of creatives. As most of them might say, *Make me well—but not that well, because I have to write, paint, play, feel.* As if normal can't include those things. Artists sometimes confuse being organized with not having feelings. What? No lamenting? No joyful dance? No spontaneous trips to the Alabama border for figs? Who wants to live like that?

Which brings me back to life, and if to life, then to death. Which brings me back to Thanksgiving, to my grandmother, to thinking deeply about her and believing that somehow, by some mystical means, I will see her again. That the essence of me will meet the essence of her and we will know each other and remember this life and our days together here on this earth. If that's not mystical, I don't know what is—that one day in the hereafter we will be there together.

There is a scene in one of my favorite novels, *Peace Like a River,* by Leif Enger, where a character "crosses over" and lives to tell the tale of what that was like. The description rang true to me, foolish though it may seem to some people who stand on the other line of belief. Maybe, upon death, they'll find something different than I will. A black hole of indifference, of nothing. Of no more. But I don't worry about that. I don't argue about it, either. And no matter what you may think or believe about the afterlife, on this side of the curtain you don't know any more than I do about what we'll find out there. We simply know what we believe, what we think, what we suspect, expect, desire.

Of course, what I think is the truth and I'm the one who's right.

Insert smiley-face here.

My grandmother was a tall, serious woman with a strong back and long fingers. They were ever-so-strong and picked quantities of cotton worthy of a man in hot Southern summer suns, year after year. But by the time I came along, the first baby of her last baby, she was no longer picking cotton. That kind of poverty was gone, and now she spent her time rocking and baking chocolate cakes. At least for me. We were perfectly content sitting quietly in one another's company as she brushed my hair, those strong fingers turned as gentle and soft as her heart was toward me.

Which reminds me of God and pilgrims and a kind of love that is perfect. Scott's scholar writing about *theosis*, that state of being one with God without being God. Of being and breathing in the presence of God, like a cloud encircling your heart at all hours of the day. In the most Protestant terms, emulating Jesus, who said he was one with the Father and that he had come to give us abundant life. To show us a way to be all of our days.

Thanksgiving, leaves, love. Pilgrims, all of us. Every one. Walking out our days, searching eBay, posting on Facebook, and watching funny cats on YouTube as we quickly pass over the news that hurts us. Another shooting, another war, another displaced child. As if a purse, a joke, a post, will save us from the noise, the fear, the flight.

I imagine God as a blanket and reach to pull him tighter, to enclose myself with a light that outshines the pain of darkness. I close my eyes and desire to be there. To remain and to carry a torch of truth forward. Then the big dog barks forty-two times. I have to go investigate what danger he has discovered. A cat trying to eat his food? A squirrel taunting him from a tree? I tell myself I can do this and not walk out of that Presence that is and was and will always be. But—*snap*—just like that, I do.

Life carries on. It gets messy. I find myself outside watching the leaves on the trees dance, tremble, cling, and fall away, and I'm alive in this moment and so grateful for this luscious, sensual life filled with light and color and this true blue sky with the wind licking away leaves by the dozens as they rain down upon me. And I think, *I'm going to die.* I know this. Not today, not even anytime exactly soon. At least, I don't suppose. Still, it's all just a passing shadow. What I wonder is this: if there be peace, where may I find it? In this world of pain, of terror and torture, where can I find this God of love I believe in? Is he hiding? Has he turned hopeless? Have we been left to our own defenses so that the weak get trampled, the poor and hungry ignored, the innocent bled to death by guilty men with hearts made of murder? As I live and breathe and write, as I drink with friends and laugh and share. As I bitch about what's troubling me, which is nothing worthy of my bitching.

I wonder how much it will take until things change. How much we will endure of our pain that we trial and trouble through. That we bury beneath our comforters and coats, our distractions and our desires. We all hide our pain from the public, hide it from our friends, from the world, from ourselves. And, in doing so, we'll hang on to it, cleave to it, feel it, focus on it, no matter what pill someone prescribes to numb the mind. Whatever answers we might discover don't seem worthy of the time it takes to ask the questions.

I close my eyes, feel the wind, hear the rain of leaves, the chickens next door scratching at the dirt, and beyond that—everything. The traffic down in Nashville, a honking horn, musicians making music in their sleep. Farther still over hills, the sound of waves crashing on a sandy beach, my mother dreaming, rolling over in her sleep, and beyond, beyond, beyond. I listen, and somewhere a baby's being born, his cry a crescendo of his arrival, and somewhere an old man is dying, taking his last breath, and somewhere someone's just now fallen deeply in love for the first time and they are full of flitter, like being born again. And somewhere good is being done in secret, and somewhere a writer is scribbling words on a napkin; an artist stirs her paints; a child, with music in her soul, holds her fingers poised on the keys. Across that mass of ocean and farther still, a soldier waits for a letter that isn't coming, and in another country a candle is being lit, a poem sketched; a woman moans, a rooster crows, a father swings a laughing child, then holds her close.

Up and beyond those dusty mountains is the whisper of unselfish prayer, and somewhere, right this minute, a heart is breaking; and somewhere a lonely person hopes for someone, anyone, to talk to. Somewhere in the soft, blue light of night, a mother rocks her newborn, singing lullabies; the baby, nestled safe, sleeps in perfect peace. And all of this—every square inch and molecule—is magic of the deepest kind.

Someday I'll leave this old, tired earth. Become like that lucky old sun, rolling around heaven all day. Maybe it will be familiar but beyond my recognition, unreal in all its dazzling glory. If everything I believe is wrong and the veil is nothing more than fairy tale, I'll be dust and nothingness. I'll be either with those I've loved or simply the echo of an energy, a dying star that takes a bow and turns out the light. In that case, I won't dismay one moment that I have believed.

People say that surely Peter stands at those pearly gates, that the streets are paved with gold, that there's a tree with twelve different kinds of fruit and the water runs so pure it's light. There is no darkness; there is no weeping. I hold that hope dear. That dream for me, and for the oceans full of passing souls who come before and after me.

In his final installment of the Chronicles of Narnia series, *The Last Battle*, C. S. Lewis delivered Lucy to heaven's gate by train. It seems to me that would be most fitting if in death there might be a portal of a place we pass through. A kind of boarding as we move from here to there. A place where we get our final ticket punched and board the train that holds our name.

35

The Whistle Calls My Name

I've just boarded a train. I'm a little weary, ready to take my seat, but then, what's that? Right there at the end? I see a man behind—is that a bar? I think it is.

He looks my way, shoots a wink as he wipes the counter down. He has a good face, a kind face. I approach the counter; there's a flicker of lights, the whistle of a train.

He pours a drink, sits it there before me. "For old times' sake," he says.

Bless him. I could use a drink. I've grown a little tired of late, and I could sit a spell. I pull up a stool, sit down, and raise my glass to him. Then I take a sip. The first sip is bittersweet, just as I expected, but with the next, the warm burn of love slides across my tongue, mingles with a little melancholy on its way down. Every sip hits a different note, like a baptism in the summer rain—holy, hot, and liquid. I gaze into the glass, measure its final taste. "Here's to life," I tell the man as I raise the glass again. He smiles; he understands.

The last small sip, and there it is, a splash of wonder, the scent of angel.

It's done now; I can feel it in my old bones. But just in case, I look around. Maybe just a little more.

"Hey, bartender? Could I get one more glass of time? One for the road, perhaps?"

He looks at me, full of glory. He polishes the counter, slow and steady strokes in circles.

"I think maybe"—I try to see out the train-car windows, but there is only darkness reflected there—"I should stay one last day to finish up a little business, a few things I've left undone? One to make apologies due a long time ago." Now he looks at me like he knows I'm just buying time, but still—

"I see, I see. The time for apologies has come and gone. Well, then, perhaps if not a full one, maybe not so much. Maybe just half a glass? Just enough to wash regret right off my skin, the residue of scarlet sin? Umm. I can see you strike a hard bargain, sir, but still, I like your smile. You look familiar, yes—you and I, maybe we are kin." He shakes his head. "You're saying no, do I have that straight? Okay, okay. Look, if not a glass, or a heavy pour, perhaps you'd consider one tiny shot." I hold my fingers just so wide and crack my eye a bit.

Just one more memory, one more moment, one long kiss hello, one last kiss good-bye.

"I see, I see. No more time for that. Time to settle up, exit into the light of this dark night. Then let it be. We're all good here." He holds his arms out, shrugs his shoulders, as if it's all beyond him. It's just the rules he follows, after all.

"Hey, it's all right. No worries, man, I understand. I'm just a pilgrim born to die. I'll tell it true, I will, no lie." I run my finger on the rim, stare into that empty that was my life. "I loved it well. I did. The good, the bad, the pleasure, and the pain—I loved it all. To the last drop." I set the empty glass back down. "And I hate to say good-bye."

A train whistle announces our arrival at our destination. The bartender points to the door at the rear end of the car. "Guess this is my stop." The door slides open of its own accord. I take a deep breath in and step down from the stool. "Okay. I'll catch you next time." I point to the open door. "Right there on the other side."

I turn back, give him one last wave; he raises his right hand, a priest giving benediction, or maybe a bedouin's good-bye.

I offer up one last wave and turn to face the door.

There is a hush, a heavy, holy silence, a waiting. It's time to end.

Oh, Great Creator, Dream Weaver of my weary soul; oh, Wild Wonder, Majestic Mystery, Lord and Maker, Father, Comforter, and Faithful Friend, please take my trembling hand.

36

A Gypsy Daughter's Dissipation

I'm helping Mother move from Panama City, Florida, to Nashville. She has reached her eighties and it's time. Actually, it's overdue. I've been trying to get her to make this move for years. So for many years this has been "in progress" and "I'm working on it." My suspicions that she was coming up with just one more thing to delay the big day when the furniture would actually be removed from that house of forty years have been confirmed more than once, and I have been frustrated to no end with her. Then I look at my daddy's picture on my desk, the one with that sly grin, that little cigar in his teeth, a bucket of crickets in his hand. It was a happy, Daddy-is-going-fishing kind of day. Thank God somebody, somewhere, took that picture and caught that moment. I look at that grin, think about the way he loved my mother. What he would be asking me to do if he could. I take a deep breath and think, *Patience, patience*. Then I call Mom on the way home and say, "Don't worry. It's all going to be okay. I'll handle it." But truth is, I'm worried. Overwhelmed about how I am possibly going to ever in this world get this huge task accomplished. Getting all the good stuff (and all the junk stuff) relocated to Tennessee seems the equivalent of the tribes leaving Egypt. All of them. I need a Moses. I need a Red Sea parted. Maybe I can grab my walking stick, drive down to the Panhandle, and stand in the road, point that stick at the house, and the junk will simply part, the treasures separated from the trash. Maybe I can point to the road ahead, and it will be cleared of those emotional barriers we are battling. It will heal my mother's possibly imposing depression; it will prevent me from freaking out, trying too hard to make everything all right. To make everything shiny and bright and good. Stardust here, stardust there. Wish I may, wish I might. And mixed up in all those worrisome to-dos and I-gottas, there is this sense, this knowledge, that my mother is leaving me. One day at a time, getting closer to the brink of that exit door. I'm not ready for her to go. I wasn't ready for Daddy. Not when he was at the end of the end, only days away from dying and I dropped at his feet, my head in his lap, trying to say everything that could not be said between my army daddy and me. We had struggled so hard to talk, like magnets that almost, but can never, touch. And I cry now when I think about how, every single time he extended an olive branch to try to communicate, I, like an idiot, would mouth something off and not realize until years later that he was trying his best to relate to me, to reach me. And in that final hour, I could feel him freeze inside with me in his lap. Not because he didn't want me there, but because he did—afraid that if he moved in the slightest or laid his hand on my head, I'd be gone. That I'd shatter like glass beneath his hand, no matter how light the touch. Or that I'd dissipate into thin air, a gypsy-daughter dream, never real at all.

No, I wasn't ready for Daddy to leave me, and I'm not ready (nor am I going to be ready) when it's time for Mom to go. I hate this losing with all my heart.

No matter how much I know it's a normal part of life, it still takes me by surprise, a gut-punch, a breathless grasping for what isn't any longer there. For *who* isn't there. I lost a part of myself when my grandmother died. I had one last conversation with her. Then she was in the hospital and they told me not to come. That the baby was little and Kansas City was a long way off. That I didn't want to see her this way. They told me she had been seeing me, having visions or hallucinating, talking to me as if I were by the bed. Then they told me not to come to the funeral because what was the point now, but that ended up being the wrong thing for me to do in the long run.

Sometimes the decisions that make logical sense will be a sudden gut-punch drop when the truth finally hits home. Logic doesn't think that a young girl should fly with a little baby to a funeral. What good now to be there for the open coffin? What good now to stand in a little chapel and hear the old refrains of "Amazing Grace," sung with the familiar family voices? Besides, it's just one young girl, one small baby, a long distance, and many dollars for a plane ticket. What good is it—except now the girl will grieve in broken sobs for years to come. What good could come from her saying good-bye to that one heart that possessed an unconditional, inescapable, impossible love for her all her known days?

There is this hole, punched through the gut, through the walls, the clouds, this hole that will not be healed even in a year when the girl goes home again and searches her grandmother's room, desperately tearing through all of her things, looking for something she can't name. Something that is her safe place. Throwing open boxes, looking under old photographs, old cards, old scarves. Smelling talcum and sweet perfume in the folded clothes, searching and searching until the girl crumbles on the floor with the realization that what she is desperately searching for is not coming back. That a beautiful old woman is gone. Buried, six feet under. And nothing is going to bring her back into this life right now.

Of course that girl was me. Is me. All these golden years later. I spent time in counseling, because five years after my grandmother died I was still grieving. I had repeated nightmares of her dying. So where was my faith then? In the same place it always was. Believing had nothing to do with me getting stuck in grieving; humans have broken places.

Even though I see this messy, broken humanity in me, I do so aspire to be more like the mystics of old and days gone by. The ones who served the world with words and light. Like those featured in *The Mystics of the Church*, by Evelyn Underhill. I trace the words with my fingers as I read them, willing them to pull me under, to help me find that space alone that is God. The one who is protected and possessed by the *uncreated light*, as Ruusbroec describes.

I want to feed the orphans, clothe the homeless, visit prisoners, fight for justice. To fight the evils of this age. And I want a pedicure, a new leather purse, and to find something stupid on YouTube to take my mind off all the good things left undone.

Fuel plumes of an airplane crisscross the sky. They are so shapely, so significant, that I think maybe the pilot is carving out a message for someone. Or maybe he's just that guy who likes to fly around a lot in our neck of the woods and he's taunting me, the way the sound of his engine does flying over the house on a clear, blue-sky Saturday morning. I can hear him dipping and diving, then soaring, and I long to be up there, complete with stupid hat and goggles, in one of those open-cockpit numbers of the early twenties. Freedom. I think so much of my life comes down to circling that word and striving to find it but still wanting that touchstone to remain at home. That place where I am always welcome, where someone's eyes light up to see me. Someone who has made my bed ready and saved me a warm plate of supper just in case I am hungry when

I arrive. Someone who stashes my favorite things, treats that will be waiting.

When I was the smallest child, right around five and six, when we had moved to Germany, I was playing with other children outside the military base housing building. The word *playing* seems strange now, since I don't remember that place as a place of play. My place was north Florida and warm sand and backwoods and cousins. Who could have fun without cousins? But in this moment I was occupied with whatever we had found to interest us for a moment. We played on the small green space that backed up on the wild German fields within eyesight of my mother should she look out the window, and also within earshot. Even three stories up she'd hear me if I called her loudly, and so she allowed me to be outside without her. I was such a well-behaved child. Really, I was. Then they appeared.

It was like an old melody. Something that called to me on some primordial level that escapes me to this day. Bells. I heard them. So did the other kids, and when we looked off into the distance of those fields, gypsies were crossing with wagons pulled by oxen. Some might say they were farmers, but why would farmers have big covered wagons and oxen that could pull all the way to the moon and back? We were children. We had no choice but to run after them. So we ran. And ran. And ran some more.

I hadn't realized it, but one by one the other kids had sensed that we were traveling too far. That we were out of range of our assigned zones. That we were no longer on government property, on base, on level playing ground. This stay-close-to-home was ingrained. Yet I, a shy child, a child afraid to fight, one who ran from bullies and preferred a warm, cozy room and books to a day of sledding that required pulling on four pairs of pants and trudging out into the snow, was still running, following the call of those bells in the distance. My mother's intuition must have kicked in. She must have been pulled as if by gravity to look out and see only the top of my head barely visible in the distance, bobbing and disappearing in whatever tall grain was growing. She called my name again and again, yet I kept running. Then, finally, this twinge of guilt, this whole relationship-to-my-mother, this duty to family first, landed on my heart. I slowed my gait, then came to a full stop, but I didn't turn around just yet. I stood watching the gypsies disappear into the horizon of grain, the bells ringing in the distance so faintly they were like a dream. I turned slowly, head down, and walked back toward a mother and dinner that would be on the table. Where my mother would not tell my father what I'd done. Where I'd lie in bed that night with wonder—starry nights and other worlds heavy on my mind.

Now I'm thinking so many things at once while I continue to watch that plane trail smoke as I'm driving home. If he's not sky-writing, he's certainly sky-painting. I watch the gold leaves shake in the wind and, there again, the moment is alive and dead and bittersweet, like this life. Then I turn up the crooked path that leads to my home of years now, and I realize I am driving through a tunnel of flame. The sun, deep and red through the trees along the ridge, has cast a peculiar light, that same light I always think of as residing in Taos. A light that becomes an actual presence because it is so intense, so ethereal, so otherworldly. The trees have possessed this light, every one of them filled with orange leaves, and they look like torches along my way. I put my foot on the brake to slow, look in my rearview mirror, and think of stopping the car entirely on this hill and getting out right then, right in the middle of the road.

No human could pass through this portal and not realize that we were driving through wonder, that our road had become a thin place, encircled by something beyond us. Don't give me a load of science jargon and explanation. Humans were created to recognize reality shifts, to feel it when the other is near.

The hills and curves of Tennessee are not the greatest of spaces to jump out of your car as you curve up along the rocks—on one side, edge; a drop-off on the other—so I continued driving, as slowly as I could while totally and completely enraptured. Then it occurred to me—

Oh, wait, this happens sometimes when you wear your sunglasses and it gives everything that glow. I reach up to pull off my sunglasses and realize I've already switched to my clear glasses—no Polaroid magic. No question about it, I was going to reach my driveway and turn right around and go back down the hill and drive up through that tunnel of fire again.

I did just that as soon as I crested the hill and hit our drive. I turned around, drove back down. Immediately. I pulled into the tiny, empty church parking lot at the bottom of our road, whipped a U-turn, and began to drive up again, but it was gone. The glow, the fire, the intensity—gone. All was normal. The sun was setting over the ridge in a red streak, the pink of the sky before it, the regular orange of the leaves. Move along, now. Nothing spectacular to see. No rubbernecking.

But it had been brilliant. And although it was still beautiful in every way, it wasn't insanely, passionately, vibrantly on fire. That's what it had been: fire. Where something extraordinary happens in the midst of our lives, and if we aren't too busy, if we aren't too blind, if we keep dialed into the divine, we find that we arrive at these places much more often in life. We see the green flashes, the shooting stars, the electric sunsets.

I think heaven is like that. This place we hope for and imagine. I think that tunnel of light is like those trees. So mesmerizing that people are drawn to it. I've never heard a story where someone had a near death experience and ran away from the light. Everyone wants to keep going. They want to keep going forever. I know I did, when I came up that hill and passed through that tunnel. God only knows how many miles I would have traveled if the light along that curving path had never ended. I might still be driving now instead of writing these words.

I'm thinking leaving this place is like that. That once we shuck the skin, as painful as that might be in different deaths, we slip from one place into another. That it is seamless once we take that step. That whatever is beautiful here is multiplied a thousand times there. Electrified. Yet I do not long to die. That's for certain. Not only because there are so many moments in this life that I relish, but also because I do believe the journey is the learning. That there are things we are meant to understand along the way. That, hopefully, by the time we reach the end of our days and we board that train at the station, we have come a long way, baby, from where we've been. It's why so many older people wouldn't choose to suddenly be twenty again. There's a lot of fun in being twenty but also a lot of nameless angst. At least there was for me. And a lot of stupidity on my part, bad choices and so forth, but life goes on and we learn—and, yes, that old adage *It's what we do with what we learn* that matters.

37

An Encounter of Mystical Proportions

Once upon a time when my sons were small, I took them by boat to the front side of Shell Island, just off the coast of Panama City. We dropped anchor, and wild dolphins came up alongside us. I had watched them roll through the gulf now for years upon years. Had watched them breach the water, riding backward on their tails, smiling and talking to me. It was the wildest thing. They once surfaced just off the shore as we held a memorial for a friend. There were many reports of the dolphins showing up at quiet memorials as tiny boats paddled out to set a passed loved one free to the sea for all eternity, and one of those reports was ours.

And we were always pleased when something moving through the water turned out to be a dolphin, usually in a pod family, and not a lone shark. I had also grown up on the beach when *Jaws* first hit the big screen, and it was the only summer I remember where people literally did not go over their knees in the water. If someone did, everyone stood there watching them swim out to the second sand bar, just waiting for them to be gobbled by the great white we were certain was on its way. So that rolling back—not the sharp, straight movement of a dorsal fin—is the signature of the dolphin and is always a welcome sight to see.

This particular time with my sons, we are anchored and our pod of a family of dolphins surface beside the boat. When their heads are sticking out of the water, they look friendly, they sound friendly, and they look approachable. They will let you feed them sardines from your hand. (Something, by the way, you should never do.) On this day years ago, I decided not only to slip into the water to swim with them, but also to allow my sons to do the same. Looking back on it, I was crazy. It didn't matter that my sons could swim like fish; the fact was, and remains, that they are not fish, and if one of them allowed a grandchild to get in the water now with wild dolphins, I would have a conniption fit. Not because dolphins are bad or I'm afraid of them, but because anything could happen. It's the old "Do as I say, not as I did." But on this day I let the boys swim, and I'm sure they are glad for it.

Here is the first thing I noticed when I got into the water, when I could see the rest of the dolphins under the water, as the gulf was in a green, clear mood: they are huge creatures. Once I could see exactly how large they were, I could calculate how powerful they were as well. I realized that we were more than vulnerable. If they didn't like us, we were toast. But we were already in the water, and while there was an element of "Oh no!" in my brain, it was overridden by a sense of "Oh wow."

The pod had a small baby dolphin with them, and we were fascinated by him. The amazing thing to me is that they were fascinated by my youngest son, who was small enough for them to realize he was a little human, and they circled around him and stared at him. It's true. We swam with them in a way that you might encounter a foreign family and sit down for a picnic together in spite of the fact that you couldn't speak one another's language. We could still communicate, and it was clearly a social call. That experience hung with me for a long, long time. There was something special about it. A lot of people who have swum with dolphins will tell you that. That otherworldly, haunting experience.

God's like that.

Hauntingly clinging, our experiences with God hover over us. I've heard tell that Mother Teresa had only one deeply personal experience with God that might have seemed out of the ordinary—whatever her own ordinary might have been. Apparently, it was enough to carry her forward for a long time and a life's work. I'll most likely never swim with the dolphins again. Not wild ones. It doesn't happen every day. Especially in Tennessee. What I long to do more than return to those waters with the dolphins, as magical as it might have been, is to swim in the deep waters of God.

Surely, no matter what depth we stand in, there is always deeper water, up until the day we die. What I long for is a type of communication that continues. That goes beyond the borders of this material world. I love what Elizabeth Gilbert said in her book *Eat, Pray, Love* about searching for God like a man with his head on fire searches for water. I love the way Annie Dillard embraces the "all" of Nature, and the way Scott Cairns searches for a deeper prayer life with all his soul. I love that Jacob wrestled with the angel, declaring that he would not let him go until he blessed him.

I think the presence of God is drawn to that wild passion, that search. As a priest told Scott, while he was on his pilgrimage to search for God with all his heart and being, "When you find him, hold on to him." I agree. That's the tricky part. I have found God. I have swum in the deep waters. I have touched the hem of something that is larger than my life and everything I know. Hanging on to that is a different thing altogether—Moses not just speaking to the flaming bush and going down the mountain, but eating the flaming bush and carrying it with him.

The ever-present burning presence of God inside me, like a fire that warms the cold and lights the dark, wet night with hope.

38

Hanging Out in the Late-Night Hacienda

*T*oday I woke up to a dusting of snow. Some years Nashville gets a few good snows, and some years it does not. This morning was our first, and it came early. The creatures all around us have apparently taken a vote, and it must have been unanimous: today will be a very quiet day. There are no roosters crowing. No braying from the donkey that lives through the woods and down the hill. The dog across the way from the blue house in the meadow isn't barking. No squirrels chatter; no birds are calling. My very own big dog is hushed and napping, the cats curled into warm spaces on clothes where they don't belong. I hear only the wind, the dry leaves rustling that still cling to the trees, the soft dripping of the melting snow from the eaves. It could be the kind of day you call in sick when you are well, keep on your pj's and get a book to read, even if you don't read. Even if you watch television thirty-six-hundred hours a day. Today you would not want to hear it. The quiet has that kind of power.

There couldn't be a better day to be a writer, to sit at this desk on this hill, to look out across the dusted ridge and contemplate this dancing swirl of words. To hear their dance and only them. To hear the beats that rest between them in the silent places. The space between the words is so important. In the space between the words we say everything. Today I am surrounded by quiet and the books of other writers, messengers one and all of truths being told and forever bearing witness to some nuance of this existence.

A few times in my life, as I grew wiser and more aware, I began to take retreats here and there. Although you don't take them so much as make them. In this life and culture, carving out one day unplugged from all we have become is like moving mountains. To carve out three or forty? That's a military operation to get yourself good and gone. There are animals to plan for and kids and husbands or wives or mail or to-do, to-do, to-done-diddly-done. It never stops. Ever. Never. Not in my world. Most likely, unless you are reading a very yellowed, dog-eared copy of this while you are on retreat in a desert place and it has been delivered to you by a camel, not in yours either. But I can tell you this: there is just about nothing that three solid days and nights of quiet and no speaking, no texting, no calls, no emails, no television, no Facebook, no Twitter, no YouTube, no LinkedIn, no Circles, no Google, no iTunes, no Netflix, no Red Box, no Pinterest, no—do you see it? How much noise possesses us? How much chatter? Chatter is okay in a kind of balanced moderation, but when our days and nights are consumed with mindless consumption and regurgitation, we might just get a little sidetracked from what's truly important. Like, *oh, let me see* ... being human. Being fully alive. I'm not sure we know what that is anymore, without our social networks and media to the left and to the right. What would we believe, think, or feel if we had no one telling us what to believe, think, or feel? To say we aren't influenced by what we are feeding ourselves is naive. We simply need to choose carefully (and straight up—your idea of *carefully* and mine might be different, and that's the way it should be). We need to allow ourselves to think and pray and listen. I can pray and listen and think while I'm playing music full throttle and running hard and fast. But it's not the same. It's never the same.

Cousin Deb says if she had to go somewhere and be quiet and not talk or see anything or anyone for three days, she'd go crazy. She would not. She thinks she would, but she wouldn't. But she might cry. That does happen when we get quiet and steady. We hear our lives talking to us. If being quiet and not talking to anyone for three days makes us crazy, then we're all running around crazy all the time anyway. We're just masking it. And the more we mask, the more we lose ourselves. And the more we lose ourselves, the more we lose each other.

I've got this weird feeling that our not losing one another is of the most critical importance. Not everybody likes everybody, you know. That's okay too. Some people just rub you the wrong way. Maybe it's me, but if not, most people get irritated by certain "types" of other people. So you just pray for them. Not all up in that *Jesus-help-them-be-more-like-me* way, just in the way of asking for good things. All good things. I used to hate going to church and hearing a sermon on loving each other and loving strangers and loving your enemies. Praying for your enemies. Those were sermons meant for me to think about other things in my life. Love, love, love, yeah—let's get over it already. Do good, be ye holy, holy, and let's go home. My resolution to pray for others changed that. Not immediately, not in a week or a month, but after a year or two or three, yeah, sometimes things change you. Not that I wasn't someone who loved and cared before; I was. Not that I didn't pray for my enemies; I did. But the loving became easier. The forgiving became easier. Most days I have to get up and forgive again. But maybe that's part of the lesson. Forgiving someone once, well, that's not so bad in the big picture. You get through it and it's done. But wrestling that thing, that pain, that lie, that betrayal, or whatever it might be, again, and again, and again—that will just flat wear you out. Or refine you like that furnace where silver and gold are perfected. You know, that's what they tell you:

"Honey, you know when you are going through hell, you are supposed to just keep on going. There's probably something you should be learning from this experience. God's just working the dross out of you."

All that biblical *in-the-furnace-and-the-dregs* and so forth. I hate that stuff. Okay, I dislike it quite a bit. I'd rather God buy me a massage so somebody else could work the kinks out of me.

But the fact is, sometimes it is a learning experience, if we see it. Sometimes we do become better and stronger in the process.

And sometimes we do not.

I have always had a bone to pick with Nietzsche. That whole *what-doesn't-kill-you-makes-you-stronger* thing.

Yes, I get it. But sometimes what doesn't kill you just makes you wish that you were dead. Flat-out. Like you have been knocked down and out so many times that getting up again has no appeal whatsoever. Without help. Sometimes from a stranger.

We are *that* connected in this life. This divine being that cast us out of the shadows of imagination and into the light of existence never intended for us to be so self-sufficient, so in control, such spiritual giants that we are beyond needing each other. And if we can't accept a hand reaching out, we will never, and I mean *never*, be able to extend one to someone else without strings of superiority being attached.

I do not mean those precious, clinging codependents who aren't validated unless you yourself are weak and needy. Most of us have had one of those people in our sphere at some point, and we remember this even if it was back in grade school. There's a difference between dependence and need. Need? See *knocked down and can't get up.* See *figuring you are better off staying down or being dead.* If we don't allow other people to see us in all our weakened glory, in our broken, human mess, then how are we ever going to take off our mask and show the world (or just one good person) the real deal behind those walls we call a life?

In the quiet place, we find ourselves. And we find God. And we find God in us. He is in me, surrounds me, and lays out a path before me. It takes the quiet for me to listen, to have sense enough to walk it.

Otherwise I look like that old *Family Circus* cartoon where little Billy takes the long way home. I'm all over the place, buzzing through life like Jeff Goldblum in *The Fly* when he was jazzed on sugar. I'm a hamster on a wheel, running as hard as I can but getting nowhere fast. So I just run harder and harder and harder, thinking that something will finally get caught up and click into place and I'll find some quiet time then.

No. Not happening. I have to jump off the crazy wheel and run as hard as I can to a quiet place and slam the door and fall on my knees and pray, *Help me be silent. Help me be still.*

39

To Cuss or Not to Cuss Is Not the Question

*T*here is an actual discussion taking place over whether or not Christians should cuss. I happen to know this. If Hindus and Buddhists and Jewish people are having this discussion among themselves, I have not been privy to it.

My mother tells me that when I was three years old, serious child that I was, she was grocery shopping with me riding in the front of the buggy, as children do, looking all of three and cute and like a little lady. My mother, dressed the way mothers dressed in public back then, stood politely in line with the other customers waiting with their buggies. Remember that this was not a time of sixteen registers with lines and music on loudspeakers and talking advertisements. The line was rather quiet; there was only the polite interaction of the customers with the cashier, the bag boy doing his job at the end of the register. Plastic was not an option, the cars had fins, and the Russians were the bad guys. The world was still in black and white, right and wrong; good and evil had a line so clear in the sand it was electric neon. Sins were darker, deeper, hidden. You had to scratch the surface to find them. But they were there, always abiding somewhere. Some of those would dive deeper when the scratching started, some would rise to the surface, willing absolution. Willing a clean slate, a new life. On this day, something must have scratched my sin, and it caused me to confess on my own accord without the slightest provocation or interrogation.

I looked straight at my mother, my hands clasped tightly to the buggy rail, my chubby little legs straddling that wire buggy seat, and began my declaration in my childhood Southern drawl.

"Mama." My big brown eyes, reflecting, contemplating; my voice loud enough to be heard clearly, distinctly. It wasn't a mumbled, halfhearted confession, but one filled with repentance, with resolve.

"Yes, honey? What is it?"

"I am never going to say *chicken shit* again."

Customers laughed in spite of themselves.

My mother, ever the queen, ever the calm cucumber, replied, "That's good, honey," and went on with her business. But she never forgot it, and of course that story was passed down through the ages like all the stories of "the babies" in the family. What has always gotten to my mother most about that story is the fact that I had been thinking so hard about this, coming to a decision on my own at that age about wanting to do good and be right.

I still contemplate those things. Since that earliest moment of wrestling with words, I've gone through stages where I cussed, and stages where I didn't. There were years upon years upon years when I didn't utter a single profanity. Then my daddy died.

He wasn't a man who cursed, although on the rarest of occasions I heard him use a word here or there; it was always within appropriate bounds for the occasion. The day I broke that cuss-free streak was right after he died and I was talking to my sister on the phone, both of us grief stricken and inconsolable. The only thing that could help us breathe again was Daddy being alive and walking the earth and within reach. But that wasn't happening. What was happening was that gut-wrenching pain that comes from being torn asunder, losing those we love to the other side before we're ready—and are we ever ready? I wailed into the phone to my sister, "I just miss him so [expletive not printable here] much I can't breathe." And I will not lie—the cussing helped me grieve, helped me pour out what I was trying to say. The circumstances were understandable.

Since then, here and there and on occasion (and sometimes more often than needed), I have in fact expressed myself in terms that are of a more graphic nature. Then I think, *I need to clean up my mouth.* I've written novel after novel without curse words in them, although *Saints in Limbo* should have had one in it but I was asked to exclude it or make the main character say *darn* instead of *damn*. I couldn't shove *darn* in his mouth with all my might, because *darn* was a lie. *Darn* made him sound stupid and made me look like I didn't know how to write about a good old boy from the South who liked his beer and chasing women and loved his momma and missed his daddy and was trying to do right and turn a corner in his life.

But there are movies that have handled that type of thing with witty aplomb. Especially old gangster movies: Marlon Brando in *On the Waterfront*. Humphrey Bogart as Sam Spade in *The Maltese Falcon* to Peter Lorre's character, Joel Cairo: "When you're slapped, you'll take it and like it." Boy, I get a kick out of that line. Rough characters. Dark worlds. No cussing. Hats off to them. Well done, I say.

One of our favorite movies, the innocent and iconoclastic *A Christmas Story*, does a terrific job of highlighting a kid's first curse word uttered aloud. The same one he had heard from his father fighting the furnace but had to eat soap for saying. But then, *The Boondock Saints* is another one of our favorite movies, and if you even think about picking up the DVD, I think it will start cussing in the store.

So cussing can be a sign of the times thing. A cultural thing. Maybe a cultural compass. But in my book that doesn't mean that it is a compass of righteousness or unrighteousness. It's a habit. Or a choice for emphasis. Gary Vaynerchuk is an international, highly paid public speaker who is a marketing guru. He uses the F-bomb onstage—a lot. But that's part of his style.

Ash Ambirge is a young, hot-potato marketing, copyediting hustler who founded the Middle Finger project. You get the idea right there, don't you? I happen to like her, although she doesn't know that because she doesn't know me. And her newsletters happen to be rude and crude, full of snark but straight to the point. And her no-beating-around-the-bush stuff makes me laugh aloud. Personally I appreciate the fact that somewhere on the internet you can read her very honest story about when she was almost murdered by her boyfriend, had no money, barely had the clothes on her back and a couple of dollars, and sat in her car in the Kmart parking lot trying to figure out what to do. She was so broken and alone and desperate that, although I don't know whether Ash is of a particular faith (or any), she laid her head on the steering wheel and tossed up a prayer out of desperation. Yes, apparently it had come to that.

She prayed for God to please send a band of angels or something to help her. But then she didn't hear anything or see anything changing in her situation. So she thought she better pull it together, get a grip, and push forward. And then she had an inspired idea to sell a seminar she would offer, which she posted immediately. And she watched in amazement as people stepped up, one right after another, and started buying tickets through her PayPal account and depositing money. *Cha-ching.* And she mightily climbed out of that hole she had been in. Ta-da and hurray.

Now, if I knew Ms. Ambirge and had the chance to sit down over drinks of any kind with her, I'd share a couple of stories. I'd tell her that I consider the "head on the steering wheel prayer" (or SWP) to be one that is officially sanctioned and approved by God. I think if the Bible had been written in this day and age, somewhere, maybe in the Book of Leviticus, they would talk about the power of the SWP and when to use it. About how, because it is so powerful, you need to use it only at certain times out of dire necessity. Not want, but need. (As in, when you are just dying to get an Italian leather bag on eBay and someone is really challenging your bid, and it's pissing you off because you know there are starving children but you really want that bag—that bag you are just certain someone's Italian grandmother has possibly prayed over. This is not the time to put your head on the steering wheel and say, "God, please, oh, please, bind that woman up who is trying to buy my bag so that I can get it for less money than I currently have in checking.") Oh, nay, nay; it might work just because the power of the SWP is somehow infused divinely by the atoms and molecules and stuff, but if it did I think you would be put on SWP restriction.

I have had two, in my whole adult life—two head-on-steering-wheel prayers. Here's the way the first one went down:

I was working in advertising sales. I was a single mom, struggling to make ends meet and was at the end of my financial rope. The "light bill," as we call it down South, was overdue and they were about to be turned off. Now, this is back in the dinosaur days of pagers. Can you imagine or remember when only doctors had pagers? I am about to walk through a door, cold-calling on a business to try to sell them advertising, but then the weight of it all hit me. I just laid my head on the steering wheel and said, "God, you see me and you know what I need. I could use a little help here."

Now check it.

Right at that moment, the pager goes off for me to call the office. I have to get out and walk into a store to borrow a phone, which I do. I call the office, and they tell me my church called and asked me to call them. Strange. But okay. I call the church. Lady at the church tells me to come by the church, that they have something someone dropped off for me. Strange. But okay. I drive to the church and go inside, and one of the priests-in-training or such comes out and passes me an envelope and says, "Here you go. See you later." That was it. He turned around and went back to whatever he was doing.

I went to my car, opened the envelope, and pulled out two one-hundred-dollar bills with a note. The note read, "This came in today, unasked for, as someone brought this in and said it was for you. Then they added, 'Smile, Jesus loves you.'" And so I did. And, yes, it was more than enough. It was the light bill plus gas and groceries.

The other SWP was more of a supernatural order that possibly did indeed involve angels. But I'll save that one for later.

The thing I would tell Ms. Ambirge (and I guess I'm telling her now) is that I believe angels did indeed visit her at that precise moment in her dark hour of need. I got what I needed at my precise moment, which was obviously developing before I prayed (but, hey, you know, divine timing—Albert Einstein and time warps and continuums and all that jazz—it's the same thing). The answer came at a moment I could tag. And, according to the story, so did Ash's answer when she was suddenly inspired to kick some marketing rear and make some money. We don't always get what we want. But sometimes we do get exactly what we need.

So back to the cussing.

As a storyteller, I can tell a lot of stories, and I can tell them in a lot of different ways. If I want to write to communicate with a particular audience, I want to use the language they understand. And while I don't want to offend anyone, or the masses, I have to step back from worrying about it.

Oh, there are camps on one side and camps on the other as to what significance such a thing plays, but I can simply tell you two things. Wait—make that three. Or maybe four.

I feel that having a character use the right curse word in the right situation is your business as a writer and your reader's business as a reader. Not to write anyone junk mail, but just to decide what they are okay with reading and what they are not okay with reading.

So chances are it's better not to cuss, but it's not better to make it the issue.

There is a deluge of good literature that Christians are not reading because it has a word here or there that they need to skip over. Sometimes we end up working so hard to clean up our mouths and minds that we whitewash them. Whitewashing is not the same as purification.

I went for years without cussing to make any kind of point at all. It worked just fine. I'm sure that, as time goes by, I'll quit cussing again. Just clean it up. Be more gracious, more giving, more of everything I aspire to be in the way of mature and enlightened and spiritual.

We choose the words we need in a season to use them. Maybe that season passes. Maybe some words have just become such a part of our popular culture that if I use them, someone thinks of me as acceptable, where before I was suspicious. That may sound funny, but it's true.

Maya Angelou was one of my personal heroes. I was able to hear her speak at Vanderbilt years ago, and she was one of those people of dignity who just amaze you. One of those people who makes it so you just want to go sit at their feet and listen. I love the fact that Dave Chappelle, who is not just smart but is brilliant (and cusses a blue streak), sat down with Maya

Angelou to have a conversation with her. Their conversation was a serious one about the N-word, which Dave Chappelle uses frequently and Maya Angelou couldn't abide. But I love the fact that they had a rational, intelligent conversation about this difference, trying to understand one another without losing themselves within.

In our current Christian community, there are a lot of camps. Unfortunately, a lot of what gets on air, radio, television, or anywhere makes the majority of Christians look like low-IQ, bigoted, self-righteous, judgmental Neanderthals. And it's not true. Flat. Out. Not. True. The spotlight just turns in that direction and the caricature of Dana Carvey's *Saturday Night Live* Church Lady lives on. Which was funny. But there is funny *Ha ha, I'm laughing from the inside*, and there's funny *Ha ha, we think you're all like that and just plain stupid.*

There are incredible books, authors, writers, artists, dancers, and musicians who would blow your freaking socks off with their excellence of passion and creativity and whom you might not know because they are hidden under genres and classifications that defy those who love literature to find them. I don't understand how any forms of art began to fall into subcategories of subcategories, when the divinity of all creation lives in the DNA of artists everywhere. We were created in the image of God, deal that hand however you like, and in that creation of being like him, so too do we create worlds upon worlds of beauty. We celebrate the story of us, of our creation, in every drop of ink, of paint, of sweat. And sometimes we cuss when we do it. But sometimes—most times—we do not. Sometimes we say prayers and anoint ourselves with holy oil, or patchouli, or Chanel, and move with reverence toward our tools and embark on a new creation.

I may cuss in the process, and my characters may cuss on occasion, as needed. Or I may not. The thing is, I don't want to be judged for it unless I have come to you for confession or counseling. And I don't need to judge others who do it. Personally, I've put myself on restriction in regard to a few words. Why? Because a few weeks ago I was cornered at dinner and pressed with questions that felt more like demands that I participate in a project I didn't feel called to do. And I was really, really hard pressed when I was tired and not expecting it, and I reacted like a wet alley cat facing down a pit bull. Growl, hiss, spit, cuss. And I dropped a word here and there in public that I didn't need to use there. Ever.

In the meantime, I prefer to see the fruit of the spirit in a person and to listen to their story. To concentrate more on what's issuing from their heart than what's coming from their mouth.

I don't think my grandmother would ever have wanted to hear this baby girl curse a word. But then, I never heard her say a cuss word until she reached the ripe age of eighty.

I guess she figured it'd been long enough. She was ready to speak her mind.

40

Christian Tribes

*T*oday's another one of those days. The kind where the clouds of the morning, that blanket of gray sky, have given way to sunshine, the soft kind that filters through a winter haze as if it's taking time out from summer's heat and hot and sweaty goodness. A rest-bit, if you will, for that great star that gives us life and keeps us orbiting in this travel of ours, slinging into the blackness of the galaxy, around and back again. Fabulously. Mind-blowing in its regularity of seasons of shadows and orbital eclipses. 'Round and 'round we go; where we stop, nobody knows. Not even the ghost of Einstein.

And it's another one of those days where my past comes back to haunt me. It happens all the time. And not the old mistakes, misjudgments, and stupids.

No, it's recent history.

Another letter from a reader of *Praying for Strangers* arrives in my box. A long one about how the book has affected someone's life and a story to go along with it that is simply amazing. A chain reaction of goodness that has been snapped and shuttered out into the world from those words and their being published. And it brings tears to my eyes and warms my heart and frightens me because—

I'm afraid I may be a girl people need, but not the girl people want. Because no matter how much they loved *Praying for Strangers* and how that book touched their lives, they will have to look up beyond its cover; they will have to see me in the context of all I am.

It's like when Carrie Underwood sang "Jesus, Take the Wheel."

My sister said, "I just love that 'Jesus, Take the Wheel' song."

"Uh-huh." I nodded, smiled. "And that's the same person who sang 'Before He Cheats,' and busted the hell out of a dude's truck with that bat."

Both were sung by Carrie Underwood. Both topped the charts and were crossover hits. Both won Grammy Awards. They came out on different albums, but back in the day, on a double-sided single—Jesus on one side, bat on the other—it would have been pretty funny.

I worry a little because I don't want any of those beautiful people who, reading *Strangers*, were blessed by it, who did the Lenten study, who invited me to speak, to be disappointed in my honesty about who I am. And I don't want any of those who might be a little different, say, who watch reality television, for instance, like *Housewives* or *The Bachelor*, to try to convince me to be like them.

"I'm not that kind of Christian."

Do you know how many times I've heard that sentence in the last few years? Countless; too many. It's become part of many Christians' vocabulary, that if they say they are a Christian, or if people for some reason assume they are, they feel it necessary to define what kind of Christian they are. But since they don't know how to do that, exactly, they just say *I'm not that kind*. Because Christians are not cookie-cutter cutouts. We are all very different. I think perhaps Christians are the ones who have the hardest time with this. As if someone's beliefs not lining up precisely with theirs makes their truth off kilter, their denomination not the best or the right one. I have a powerful feeling God's criteria are a little different.

But it's not so easy with this contemporary Christian concept. We have gotten confused in our own right. There are contemporary Christians and progressive Christians and conservative Christians.

There are Christians who listen to Fox News exclusively and Christians like a friend of mine, who told me heatedly last year that he hated Fox News "with such a passion that [can't print], that they should [can't print]...judgment day [can't print]...hellfire..." and so on. I have friends and family on both sides of this media fence. There are Christians who think Jon Stewart is hands down the sexiest man who was ever on television. And I'm talking young, blond, sassy Christians. And there are Christians who probably think Stewart is part of those wanting to eradicate Christians from the planet. What to do with a religion that possesses both those kinds of people? People singing "Give Peace a Chance" and Christians sporting gun racks and NRA bumper stickers. Protesting and passive Christians and angry Christians tuned into "talk radio" programs that seem to be fueling the madness.

One day, in a doctor's waiting room, I watched someone in the lab turn the television from Fox to CNN. Then someone sneaked in and turned it back. And then that other person came back and switched it back again.

Personally, I like the BBC.

Dan Wakefield wrote *The Hijacking of Jesus* years ago. And there are a ton of books that have followed. Matthew Paul Turner stirs it up big time in *Our Great Big American God*, pointing to the possibility that Americans have created God in their own image by examining our history. I'm interested. He hooked me because I'm American. And there is just as much assumption by many people about who Americans are, exactly, or what we are like, as there is about the South and Southerners. As there is about Christians and Christianity.

In the meantime, no one is getting to know anyone because we have too many labels to fight through. Or to project. Flags to wave. Lines to draw in the sand. We may need to swallow some assumptions and introduce ourselves. To the people we already know, for the first time. No false faces. No fabricated facts. No lies. No zip codes. No political barriers.

It occurred to me just yesterday in the midst of all our political turmoil that if we woke up tomorrow and the words *Democrat* and *Republican* had been magically removed from the dictionary and our vocabulary overnight, washed from our memories, we wouldn't know who to hate or why. Not with a reactionary immediacy. We would have to carefully consider the issues, read about and listen to the people running for office. Make determinations based on intelligent research, not labels. But, even more important than the voting issues, if that were possible, would be that our neighbors and coworkers, friends and family, would no longer wear those labels as well. We would have to have real discussions, honest conversation over issues about education and taxes, infrastructure and trade. Imagine a table where people could sit down to eat, have discussions without predisposed prejudice.

I think there should be prayer that could be said at our tables and over our food, in the morning over our homes, and in our cars. Something we could say in the deepest recesses of our hearts.

And not everyone is going to receive something from me. Not a story, not a prayer, not a cup of cold water. But they might from you. And vice versa. We are not created the same. Equal, but not the same. We aren't meant to be identical.

41

A Coat of Many Colors

There are Christians who believe in dancing and Christians who believe in not dancing—instruments; no instruments. King James; Amplified. Wine; grape juice. I've never seen so much judging and backbiting and eggshell-walking in my life. And I think it's all distracting people a little from that whole *walk like Jesus did* thing. Love like Jesus. Be like Jesus. Then you get into someone saying that the Bible was written a long time after Jesus died. You don't know that any of it is true. We have the camp that declares that every single word of the Bible has to be taken literally as interpretation, and the camp that says the whole thing is just a guideline for inspiration. Just skip the parts that don't apply or gel the way Grandma believes. Embrace Psalm 23 to your dying day, but skip over all the ones where David is wanting God to pluck somebody's eyes out or tie them to the stake and let ants eat them to bones. We have been so busy bottling God in America that you can go to a Christian bookstore and buy just about any version of Jesus you want. Bobble-headed Jesus? Check, got that. Jesus soap-on-a-rope to wash your soul white as snow? Check, got that one too. I don't know, I really don't know the answers to the questions that plague us about our morality and our ethics. I think we have never addressed the root cause of so many of the secret ills that have beset us for ages upon ages.

42

The Death of Desire

(A letter to an old friend recently divorced)

Dear Donna,

I'm so sorry to hear about your divorce. To say I've been there or you'll get through this is of no use. What does that mean? We all go through things and go through them differently. Same recipe, same ingredients, but the variation is limitless. What I do know is that your heart is broken. What my experience tells me is that time, eventually, will heal some of the hurt. Or maybe numb *is a better word. The adage "time heals all wounds" seems silly to me. No, time does not. Time cannot. But in time, eventually, we turn a corner and we laugh again. That counts for something. Knowing that the road continues and that moments of joy lie nestled just over the next hill on the horizon.*

Maybe something that is more universal is the agreement that forgiveness is a good thing. A necessary thing. I keep thinking about the words of Jesus saying to forgive someone seventy times seven. Basically, that every time a brother asks to be forgiven you forgive and go on again. My question is what if someone never asks for forgiveness—or at least never asks sincerely, having accepted responsibility for the damage that's been done? What then, my friend? As you can see, I still struggle with this every day.

I had a special night this year when I prayed during a full moon for everyone—it seemed like everyone in the world but certainly for all in my neighborhood—with such a sincere and loving heart. In that moment I felt renewed. I felt like this forgiveness hurdle I had jumped was a permanent one. I was wrong.

I find myself moving into these stormy places on some days. It's as if I have put my hand under a rock in the field of my soul and found residing there this hard lump that is unforgiveness. Where I have purposed to sow peace, I rustle leaves of my minutes and find the seeds of anger residing in the garden that is me. My prayer then is Deliver me, O Lord, from the wilderness that is my soul. Where the demon that torments is the shade of memories, layered upon layer, in my unforgiving mind. *The anger that pulses in my blood surprises. My lips full of prayer one day, then fallen from the grace of all of that the next. I fall to my knees with this pain, this broken heart, that resurrects itself at my own hand, turning over memories better left buried.*

These feelings, this shade of righteous anger at being wrong undeserved, is a cut that still bleeds. I see the small of it, that unforgiveness. From the great view that is God's I understand the tiny, ordinary life that is born of carrying that unforgiveness in my bag. The tight walls that can enclose my soul, brick by mortared brick, from this pain I won't lay down. I think I'm free, but then I dream of smoke and wake to find my skin still singed with all that was and is no more. The vows that were my truth are nothing but ashes and dust.

Know that when this anger left unspent finds you, it will indeed pass. I know your heart well and all its goodness. The depth of your perpetual hope in all that is kind and full of light. You have a spirit that is indomitable. Your true friends know that. They are the only ones who matter.

So, while time doesn't heal all wounds, it does provide a way for you to have perspective. A map that seems to light up and lead you through all the twists and turns that have brought you here. Pilgrim's Progress indeed. Doesn't it all get back to feeling like a pilgrim on a quest? For love. Safety. The holy grail of happiness. As the Subdudes sing, help is on the way. I fully believe in that help. That it comes at the oddest moments when we least expect it. Through an odd post on Facebook. An email from a friend. A strange postcard in the mail. I pray that the help you need arrives the way you find it. In a way you won't miss the message, that it will be timely and be the balm to your soul you need.

Stay in the light even in the midst of your heartbreak. Surely, your daybreak is on the horizon.

Your friend now and always,
River

43

Porn and Popcorn

*I*ncest and abuse has been a hushed-up hush-hush from the beginning of time, whether it was a Catholic priest or a backwoods pastor, or somebody's daddy-uncle-cousin-neighbor-down-the-road. But I have a feeling you are never, ever going to see that one rolled out in the major spotlight like you will abortion and gay marriage and all the other insane topics of conversation. Not that they aren't worthy. But there are one million children currently being exploited by the global commercial sex trade every single year.

Here are a few alarming statistics: fifty-two percent of Christian men and twenty percent of Christian women are addicted to porn. Not that it matters if porn watchers are Christians or not, but the Christian faith doesn't support the watching. Who knows, maybe those statistics and that study are off base. Regardless of what study, what numbers, you find, methinks something very evil has slithered right in while we were sleeping. It's so easy. One pop-up ad, one click of the button, and we've gone down the rabbit hole. Something seen that can't be unseen, which strangely creates the desire to see more. In a true "dark side of the force" kind of way.

If those pornography statistics are even anywhere close to

the truth, then we have a lot of closet watchers. Watch a little porn in the dark on a Saturday night, get dressed for church on Sunday morning. Watch a little porn on Tuesday, go to a prayer breakfast on Wednesday and talk about how we are just going to have to do something about the disintegration of the American family as a healthy unit. Turn a blind eye to the child porn industry that has grown to three billion dollars, and better turn the other blind eye to the fact that fifty-eight percent of those sites are in America, the land that I love and that my daddy and my sons fought to protect. They were fighting for our freedom for better reasons than this. 'Cause when I think about the fact that many of us may be living judgmental lies and presenting Christianity as a *my-cup-of-Christian-is-better-than-your-cup-of-Christian*, I get a little ruffled.

There are major controversial issues at play, but I think they only scratch at the surface of some deep-down nasty that's pretty much being ignored. So while we are busy fighting about whose Jesus is the real Jesus, all hell is breaking loose behind closed doors. Marriages are destroyed. Women are violated. Children are molested. And lust is set loose to roam and devour in a growing frenzy. Sex is a beautiful, cosmic, awesome thing. Sex polluted by porn is a tragic unraveling of standards, ethics, and humanity.

44

Where We Begin Again

One of my favorite books to use for centering myself into what is holy and important after I have binge-watched an entire season of something frightening and artistically superior such as *True Detective*, season one, is the small book *Always We Begin Again*. The writer, John McQuiston II, expresses such a great humility that it astounds me. He is an attorney in Memphis, an Episcopal, and more gifted with divine inspiration and insight than even he seems capable of understanding.

After his father's funeral, someone offered him a word of wisdom from *The Rule of Saint Benedict*. This is a great work written by Saint Benedict, but the rules of the Benedictine way of life are not easily read and applied by those living the everyday life of people not committed to the monastery. Mr. McQuiston set out to write the rules in an easily accessible little book that everyone could read and incorporate into their daily lives. Now celebrating its twenty-fifth year, the small book is available with a foreword by the great spiritual author Phyllis Tickle. It's one that I would recommend for anyone to keep handy, with a promise that reading it will most likely rebalance your perspectives in such a way that it also rebalances your life in the process.

For instance, one of the rules of the order is a balance between work and rest, study and prayer, exercise and sleep. In a world where we are plugged into devices all our waking hours down to the moments, there is a simplicity in the order of these days that encourages me to put down my phone, my texting, my emails, and walk away from it all to embrace focusing on the task at hand. To engage socially with others face-to-face. To have lunch when possible with someone or in community. Then to return to rest and to work.

Now that my mother has moved in with me, I find that working and concentrating at home is more challenging. Some days it's downright difficult. There are unforeseen interruptions that come in the way of a simple request. Or simply by my own encouragement. It's much easier on some mornings to have coffee with Mom and watch a rerun of *Columbo* than to hit the keys and produce. I can justify this by saying to myself, How many more episodes of *Columbo* will I be able to watch with Mom at this age? But the work must go on. So, whether the interruptions are initiated by Mom or invited in by my own accord, the results are the same: fewer words on the page.

For many artists, an issue with ADD is apparent to some degree, and mine is no more than any writer I know. I struggle with getting into the chair, putting my hands on the keys and my eyes on the screen. Once there, I have no issues. That is unless I take a break, or wander downstairs for a cup of coffee, which can result in my having a cup of coffee and watching *Columbo*. Because of my struggle not to be distracted, it is easy for me to rush downstairs to grab something for lunch, see if Mom needs something or is ready for lunch, and dash back upstairs to have lunch while I work on the computer. In *The Rule of Saint Benedict*, having lunch in community is an important part of the day. This does not mean in a semi-solitary setting with all my friends on Facebook. When I incorporate reading *Always We Begin Again* into at least my weekly meditations, I concede to this fact. I slow down as I prepare lunch. I sit down with my mother and make conversation. I eat a little slower. I include her in that part of my life. Likewise, I contemplate that balance when I return to work instead of convincing myself that, obviously, I've flushed the day because I've taken a break. I have odd ways both as an artist and as a human of derailing myself into darkness, of seeing my opportunities for engagement as nothing more than attacks on my literary pursuits. This makes it so easy to jump straight to blaming the unseen monster of life's demands and provides the perfect excuse for poor performance. Back to the balance. It takes practice. It takes beginning again each and every day, forgetting what is past and letting our mistakes die and bury themselves in yesterday.

I think I need this realigning with myself and God every second of every day. And I'd be satisfied if I pulled it off just once a day. Closing my eyes and listening to the song that is my life and simultaneously, inherently, all life. As if I could stand still and look at a drop of rain clinging to a blade of grass, intently seeing it until I see my reflection there and know that I am in that drop of water, and so is God, and in that way we are one. If I could only operate from this place, surely all would be well with my soul.

Anne Lamott shares a story in one of her collections of essays, *Plan B: Further Thoughts on Faith*, about a pastor at her church encouraging the children to put themselves in a type of time-out where they sit quietly and listen. Then he asked them what they heard. Some said cars, others birds, one a radio. Then a child spoke up and said, "I hear the water at the edge of things." I agree; I am going to listen for that water at the edge of all things. For truly that must be the beginning and the awakening of my soul.

45

The Boondock Blessing

*L*et's go to the movies. I am a lover of the silver screen. A movie buff. A bonafide geek of the film world. What inspires me, makes me want to fight the good fight, may not be the G-rated, happy, family film.

Sometimes the great message of the light comes through the dark places. *The Boondock Saints.* Twin brothers. Catholic. Dedicated to communion and confession. Through a little misunderstanding, they end up defending themselves and killing some bad guys in the process. And taking some money. Which they end up donating to the church. And at the encouragement of a friend of theirs who operates outside the lines of the law, they decide that, yes, they will find the bad guys—the ungodly porn makers and dealers and lowlifes—and take them out of this world, usher them into the next. It is a violent film. It is understandably cathartic, like the Charles Bronson film from years ago where he took the law into his own hands. It's something we can't do, because we never know when to stop. Because the lines become blurred between who is right and who is wrong. Because, ultimately, those of us who believe also believe that the judgment day that is to come will far outweigh any that we can impose. I'm not talking about the law, the court, the argument for or against the death penalty, but about when we take life outside the walls of the laws we've set to protect and defend us. Does the system break down and make mistakes? You bet it does. That's why movies like *The Boondock Saints* develop a cult following. We want to take on the evil of the world like Bruce Willis in *Die Hard I, II, III* and win one for the good guys. I think it begins with us deciding to be the good guys. Not to buy into the lie that everyone does it. Or just this one little click. Can I love the world and hate just a little bit? Can I love the world and stay silent against the wrongs? Remain still instead of standing up for the weak and innocent? The displaced and the downtrodden?

From films like *Field of Dreams* to *Cinderella Man*, movies have taken to the big screen to inspire and illuminate. The manners in which they do so are as varied as the books we read. What inspires one deflates another. What gives support to all that we are and the best of what we can become may be *Star Wars* for some and *The Shack* for others. The beauty of this is that the power of story threads through all these things. Finding something redeemable in a comedy that can be rude and crude like *The 40-Year-Old Virgin* is easily within the scope of God and my neighbors.

That magical light on the screen in the dark has been my secret salvation for some time, this connection I feel to the deeper meaning of things when a story captures me, be it on a printed page or on the silver screen. Granted, I could delight in something as silly as the Three Stooges when I was a kid. Nothing is more redeemable than a good laugh. But laughter is good medicine, and if ever the world needed a good laugh in the middle of a constant newsfeed of terror and destruction, it is now. But beyond the laugh, I love all of the places that we find where we can connect with the universal experiences we all share. Those pitter-patter moments of butterflies at first love or at the edges of new love. Our Hallmark Channel moments that I might find a little too neat, too sweet, too easy. But give me *Touched by an Angel* any day of the week.

Recently I had the experience of going to see *The Shape of Water*. It was one of those special treats known as the Artist Date, popularized by Julia Cameron's *The Artist's Way*. I had determined I would take myself to the movies. (This is the idea behind the Artist Date: that you give yourself time and space alone to enjoy some activities where you are not laboring to create art.) I sneaked away from my life and all its demands, bought a ticket to a matinee at our new twelve-plex with actual easy-chair recliners, bought a drink and a popcorn. I took my seat just as the lights were dimming to dark. This is the perfect time to take your seat in a theater because it seems the world has waited for you and the curtain will now rise right on cue following your entrance. And so it did.

The Shape of Water is magical realism. It won Picture of the Year at the Academy Awards. It is not everyone's cup of tea, as it involves a sea monster, a mute woman, a gay neighbor, a pill-popping government bad guy, and so on. I don't care for nudity in movies, and it has some. However, something about the movie spoke directly to my soul and broke my heart. Fifteen minutes into the movie I was crying. An hour into the movie I was still crying. Near the end of the movie I was sobbing, although I was trying to do so quietly. The girl waiting with the broom to clean the theater looked at my tear-streaked face and said, with a look of concern, "Take care." I passed the restroom but didn't stop. I was afraid that if someone spoke to me with kindness, I'd have a breakdown. I left through an emergency exit, went straight to my car, and drove home still sobbing. Went to bed.

This is the power of story at its very best. When it touches the unseen edges of what has been shaping and shifting in us all along. When it expresses something for us that we have not been able to express for ourselves. This movie was about love and monsters, and it just wrecked me. Because it said something to me about true love and the losing of it that I haven't been able to express myself.

The story that affects you, moves you, speaks to you, is the movie you were meant to see. So incredible is this gift of story-telling and story-catching. This silver screen weaving a tangible thread to the unseen emotions and experiences in us that desire and yearn to be acknowledged, released, embraced. This exchange so powerful, like a kiss from God that says, "I see you. And I understand."

46

Body Surfing the Astral Plane

Some of my experiences in life, as well as my dreams, fall into the category of Strange. But as George Johnson writes in *Fire in the Mind: Science, Faith, and the Search for Order,* "We try to explain the strange in terms of the familiar, but sometimes it just won't stop being strange." That's how I feel when trying to recount events or make sense of dreams.

Sixteen years ago, I got up early to pray, as was my custom. The kids were sleeping, so I loved to take advantage of the quiet for prayer time. It was what I considered taking time to hang out with the presence. Although prayer was a part of that time, it was only a portion. It was more like hanging out with an old friend.

On this particular morning, I was sitting on the sofa in the living room in the quiet, reading, praying, contemplating, when I thought, *I am sleepy.* Sometimes my teenage sons would decide at eleven o'clock at night they were in the mood to talk, so I would be up late. Anyone who has been a parent to a teenager knows that the time to talk to your kid at that age is when the kid will talk to you. Although I was up early, I had also been up late. I lay over on the sofa and was out like a light.

Immediately I began dreaming. I was driving my car, which I parked at a warehouse, got out, and walked in. The warehouse was filled with wonders and treasures. I was alone but completely unafraid, although I was walking through this large warehouse on my own. I can still hear my footsteps as I took each step. See the dust particles floating in the air, caught by the sunlight streaming through windows that were high up and ran along the walls, too high for anyone to look in but able to catch natural sunlight. I became overwhelmed with a thought that I had been gone for a very, very long time. That my family would wake and find me gone and not know where I was. That they would be very worried. This thought distracted me from focusing on the things I was seeing: furniture that looked as if it had come from Bombay, stalls overflowing with beautiful items. Then I looked down at my watch. Instead of the one I wore daily, it was a very expensive-looking gold watch. One with four hands instead of two.

The ancient Greeks had two words for time. I think that was wise of them. There was *chronos* time, which followed the chronological time of things. What I would consider man's time. And there was *kairos* time, something a little harder to define. Time that is more akin to a season or a happening. Something you might consider God's time. I was on God's time. When I realized this, I was immediately, completely at peace. My *hakuna matata* moment. No worries. Time was indeed relative and all was well.

I walked through the warehouse, paying close attention to the details of the things I was viewing. As I was walking out, I saw my grandmother. She was dressed in her Sunday best and smiling. She tossed me something, and I threw up my hand and caught it. I caught it in my right palm and closed my hand around it. Then, with a sudden sensation of a physical rush, something akin to the moment a roller coaster begins its decent of the largest hill, I woke up.

As illogical as it seems, my first thought was, *I'm back!?* Then I wondered what my grandmother had thrown to me. What I had caught so perfectly.

In some circles, the astral plane is considered to be the place where the spirit realm exists. Or somewhere between this earth and the final destination. A realm where angels travel and which some humans, through meditation, can practice traveling to at will. I have never been interested in surfing the astral plane any more than I've been interested in dropping acid or eating mushrooms. I have never wanted to "take a trip" without leaving the farm. This is for very logical reasons. I've never wanted to experience a bad trip or hallucinate. Nothing about this seems charming or desirable to me. Likewise, trying to test the waters of traveling outside my body seems like a bad idea. It would be just like me to take a wrong turn and not make it back to my body in time and be stuck somewhere, like having a flight canceled and being stuck at a crowded airport. Forever.

Yet this sensation happened. It has never been repeated. I spent years trying to figure out what mysterious thing I caught in that strange, surfing dream. Until the day would come, years later, when I needed it most and it would materialize before my eyes.

47

The Company We Keep

C. S. Lewis and Tolkien met every week in a pub to discuss literature and their works in progress over pints and pipes. It all sounds so nattingly charming. The story goes that people would try to get a table nearby just to eavesdrop on their amazing conversations. Imagine such great talks about literature and God and faith and their works in progress. Then they both turned their words into works of art that have stood the test of time. I read the C. S. Lewis tales to my youngest son when he was little. Night after night we picked up where we had left off, and I was as captivated as he was. The wonderful line of Mr. Beaver's, a whispered "Aslan is on the move," has become synonymous to me with being struck by something that says to me God is alive and apparent in our world. The beauty of the character in *The Voyage of the Dawn Treader* who fell asleep in the dragon's lair only to awaken and discover he had become the dragon. What incredible imagery and allegory. How often we too are bound by greed, caught up in the thing that sparkles and in the midst of our own self-righteous sense that we have been wronged—and cuddle tighter to that thing. In this case it was the dragon's treasure. Ultimately, the boy is delivered by Aslan himself, who helps him shed his scales and become a boy again. Someone wrote that it is in fiction that we discover the deeper truths, and I agree. It is the way story illustrates and brings home the message, guiding us along, then imprinting us so that the stories are not forgotten.

Likewise, with Tolkien's work I found a home. I read *The Hobbit* and *The Lord of the Rings* in ninth grade. I traveled to visit my aunt and left the light on until two in the morning, so captivated by Middle Earth and the evil that challenged the characters as they tried to reach the fires of Mordor. Aunt Kate believed that too much reading was unhealthy, so she resorted to pushing the lawn mower back and forth under my window at seven a.m. to teach me not to read all night. It didn't work. I stayed in the books that summer. It's something now to imagine that work in progress and in discussion for ten years as it progressed.

That kind of patience doesn't appear to be congruent with our current society. Contracts demand production. Sometimes fans could forget what isn't constant. But there remain those authors like Donna Tartt and Charles Frazier who are capable of spending ten years bringing a story to life. I wonder if they feel behind? I wonder if people in their families look at them and shake their heads, thinking, *If King and Grisham and Ellison can do this, why can't you?*

For the Inklings, hanging in the pub having a pint and discussing God must have influenced them to the core. Their work was infused with God. Apparently, it matters what company we keep and what conversations and influences fuel our lives.

48

We Are Lost in Translation

*E*very day there seem to be new reports. An explosion here, a crash there, the list of the injured and the dead always mounting. The parents holding their children. Children clinging to dead parents. Images captured and shot around the world, and most of us are left with the question of what to do, guilt about what goes undone.

Children are dead, gassed in Syria. I worry about the mortgage. Think what it means to be American. To see that intervention is supported. That it is both championed and argued. I sweep my porch and mop the floor.

Tonight one of my grandsons will spend the weekend. We will bake a cake, read books, draw pictures. Tomorrow we will go to the bookstore for story time, sitting in a circle while we snack on Cheerios. And the music of the world will play all around us. The wars will rage. I will possess this life while others are losing theirs. I don't know the answers; I don't even know the right questions.

Faith breaks in among the ruins. Still. In spite of. Those children, their pale faces, tiny bodies held in their fathers' arms. One father's face is looking down, so I cannot see the expression. Shock or sadness, heartbreak or madness. I want to go to chapel. To light a thousand candles. To pray for resurrection. To ask God not to let my heart grow cold with indifference, shut down from the pain of a faraway anguish I cannot extinguish. Or to grow angry, to fill with hatred at the evil so that the evil then lives and breathes in me. I don't know what to do other than speak more kindly to my mother. Make her tea, kiss her cheek, listen to her stories. To walk with my grandson and search for the habitats of creatures under stones upturned. In light of those lives lost so young, so soon. To pray that surely angels stand at the ready to receive the dead from acts so cruel. When darkness grows and threatens to engulf us, surely the light must shine so brightly it ignites, spreading among us a hope that doesn't make any logical sense: that for each child lost, another will be born who will grow and live in peace.

When I bow my head tonight, I pray that my faith writes a new story of our future. One I can believe in. Where something human emerges from the chaos of the news. Fake news, real news. News be damned. No one is saying the real things that will matter when ratings have fallen by the wayside. That now we live. That now we die. That now we bleed and crave and seek and hurt each other when the healing is within our reach. We are a great people. Within our borders and beyond. We are a great nation and a great population. We have the answers if only we would shut up long enough to find them. To sit down and listen. Not only can our anger, which is so easily ignited in these times, but extinguish it with a powerful desire to utilize that passion for something good. The diatribes run amok, words we can all spew at one another that change no one's mind. Something has shaded our thinking. Something has invaded our hearts. I know it. I am too quick to anger over political positions. My rage from one to one hundred runs in overdrive. We hate the *they*s, but who are *they* but we? The other side of us.

I have a suspicion that my friend Shellie leans to the right. She suspects I am left of center. If we were stranded together, I would break the last bread we had and share. Shellie would eat. Then I would.

The fact is, you have never seen people so alike in the strangest of ways, as if we were sisters by birth, but also divided in ways we don't speak of. Because we value our friendship and respect the faith of one another. She knows I am as devoted as she is. And likewise. Her heart is true, as is mine. She prays, I pray, we pray.

In the midst of all this insanity that has beset us, although Shellie could argue bullet points—as could I—when I think of us, I realize it is when we lean together that we are the strongest, that we are unstoppable. If we don't talk White House and instead talk feed children, find clean water, visit those in prison, heal the sick. When we talk truth that is undeniable and goes beyond the boundaries of time and space and political geosphere and our last forty days or next one hundred years—we are bold and believable to the bone. It is that thing in us, that heart, that belief, that I recognize and call upon in these days of increasing darkness. As she cheers me on to write another Southern gothic novel, as I cheer her on to write anything, do anything, that is what I want to bottle, the essence of that—and pour it in the well that waters all our spirits. Something forged in fire and forgiveness. There is a larger picture here. And there is an evil dark and whispering that coils about us in trickery of right or left. In my best moments, when I know I am operating from a peaceful place, I know this.

It is this experience with Shellie that lets me look out at any audience, congregation, readership, the world, and realize we are not unique in our opposing thoughts nor our exact sameness. The world too has its passionate difference, which lives in every neighborhood and state. But the vehemence with which we conduct conversations on Facebook or over tables must end now. There are greater things at stake than a thousand likes. The great obstacle is not the hate that is from a coworker or on Facebook or a neighbor; it is the obstacle that the hate and intolerance grows inside of us. A secret vine that is silent, but, like that Southern kudzu on my land, will cover everything until you can't recognize what lies beneath. A car? A house? There is nothing now but kudzu. So too what once we seemed to be, individuals with opposing parties, opposing views, which all brought about a kind of balance in the end, resulted in a sustaining democracy, has tilted until we are becoming unrecognizable to ourselves.

This is my mirror. The faster I become angry, the quicker I am to speak and not to listen, the closer I am to reaction rather than understanding, the more of me I've lost to mass hysteria and some control I can't finger but expect is evil. There is something about my speech, my quickness of all-knowing, that makes me feel, in retrospect, like a puppet. Makes me wonder who pulls these strings that are my life. What part am I playing, and to what good end or dark intent? If each side of the opposition believes it serves the better good, what are the odds that someone is right? Fifty-fifty? But if I am on one side and Shellie's on the other, suddenly those odds change, because I love Shellie. I don't want to be her enemy. I am protective of the "we" of us. Not oppositional. Not choosing sides. Not on the winning or losing team.

Oh, enemy mine, I pray that in this moment in time, we find a common thread for our survival.

49

A Labyrinth in the Twilight

*F*ifteen years ago, I moved to Nashville by divine inspiration. The first place I stayed was at Penuel Ridge Retreat Center, a small ecumenical retreat that affords a wonderful place to rest and ponder. I was presenting at the Southern Festival of Books for my novel *The Gin Girl* and had a few extra weeks to explore the city.

Penuel Ridge has a day room that is excellent for writing or reading, featuring a small but exquisite library. There I found works of Merton but also of O'Connor. What caught my eye at the time was a book on labyrinths, which I wasn't familiar with. The book highlighted the history and possible positive things that could come of walking this circular path that has one way in and the same way out—unlike a maze, which has many options and is designed to be confusing in that it is challenging.

The resident manager of Penuel explained that there was a labyrinth in Nashville at St. Mark's Episcopal if I wanted to walk it. Yes, I did want to walk it—felt bizarrely pulled to walk it. By the time I found the church, which I now know to be in Antioch, the sun was setting. I parked the car, walked into a field, and there it was. This labyrinth. Flat stones laid out: a one-way path in, same path out.

While the labyrinth is not designed to be confusing, it is designed to be a journey. The labyrinth design has been discovered around the world, carved on stones and caves from all cultures and geographical locations. It was eventually adopted into the Christian culture as a way for the devout to make a pilgrimage when they could not actually travel to other locations.

The cathedral in Chartres, France, is the mother lode of these. People make pilgrimages to this place. San Francisco has one in the United States at Grace Cathedral, where the labyrinth gained huge popularity through their work in spreading the gospel of labyrinth walking. Many churches have begun to add a labyrinth to their grounds when possible. Hospitals have likewise begun to add labyrinths, realizing the health benefits gained from this short meditative walk.

While there are guidelines, there is probably no wrong or right way to make this walk. You can go on guided labyrinth walks, and St. Mark's Father Beasley offers one twice a month on a Saturday. Guided would be good. The word of advice I had received was that usually people sit a moment and decide on a question they want to focus on for which they are seeking an answer. I am always seeking answers to everything, so that was easy. For this particular walk I was starting with something small: my purpose in life.

So there I am, and there is the labyrinth. There is no one at the church. I think it was Friday night. The church and the labyrinth are off the main road, and as I begin my walk the word *secluded* comes to mind. It's growing darker. Quickly. I am not in a religious, spiritual, holy mood. I am getting slightly paranoid. I don't travel with a gun. I am alone. I don't know Nashville. It took me three hours to find this place. I just want to get this over with as quickly as possible.

Into the labyrinth. Walking, walking, zigging, and zagging. A labyrinth looks deceptively small. The design is laid out so that sometimes you come very close to the center, which is the objective, only to be led far away on the next turn, almost back to the outside. This pattern continues, and I continue following it and wanting to get through, get in my car, and get back. Finally, I am in the center. Bam. Center of labyrinth. Check that box. I stood there for all of a minute, maybe, and thought, *Nothing is happening. I don't feel anything, hear anything, and no great epiphanies. I'm out of here.*

Walking the labyrinth out, walking the labyrinth out. It sure is getting dark. It's nightfall. I'm alone. This was stupid. No one could even hear me. I shouldn't have come. Walking the labyrinth out, walking the labyrinth—then there is the last stretch and I am walking out of the labyrinth, and it happens. The moment I step outside the labyrinth is like walking through some invisible gate, and the spirit of God falls on me. I'm not going to bother trying to disguise it as something else.

When I took that last step, when that blanket of something certain fell on me, I turned back around and realized I had found my way to the heart of God. This is the experience. That we might walk, that we journey, that the heart of God is there always waiting. It is the place we enter into, then take what we find there back out into the world. Over and over again, until the world is full.

50

A Simple Molecular Manifestation

There is a romance to time travel. It transfers easily to the big screen and the page. H. G. Wells's book *The Time Machine* left its mark on me. The loose adaptation that became *Time after Time*, starring Mary Steenburgen, captivated me with its cuteness. *Somewhere in Time*, with Christopher Reeve and Jane Seymour, explored the notions of time travel as love story. The episodes of *Star Trek* that featured the away team caught in an earth of the past, Spock's ears covered with various hats and beanies, were some of the most popular. Even the holodeck vacation episodes of *Star Trek: The Next Generation* were ultra cool when they featured a flash to the past of gangsters and flappers.

There is one great time travel experiment that has eclipsed anything I've witnessed on screen or read on page. My grandmother had died over thirty years ago when she managed to send me a token that was over fifty years old.

When I had to tell my mother that I would be leaving my marriage, it was one of my most difficult conversations. It was one that I knew would cause her an extreme amount of anxiety and worry, for multiple reasons. Causing someone who is eighty to be worried raises a special kind of concern. I was at a loss for words. But it was a story I needed to tell.

My mother was living part of the time in an apartment we had rented for her. It was furnished by my friends from their various treasures and local yard sales. An old table here, an extra television there. It all came together to create a great home away from home for her. It was a complete surprise as she walked through the door and found herself set up to keep house, with dishes in the cupboards and sheets on her new bed. Her actual furniture was all in the home in Florida. The house in Panama City was in the process of being put on the market to sell, but going to market seemed to be taking a very long time. It was all a journey.

The plan had been to sell the house and for her to live with me. All of the plans had entailed moving onto the land recently purchased and renovating a house on the property. Now I was going to show up with bad news that would pull the rug out from under all those plans. And I knew the effect that was going to have on her.

When I entered the apartment, Mom was in her rocking chair. I sat down on the floor on the opposite side of the large, round coffee table that had been a Craigslist find. Mentally, I was going through my checklist of ways to possibly break the news without causing her to have a stroke.

"I have to tell you something," I began.

Her phone rang, and, distracted by the call, she answered and began to explain to someone on the other line that I had come to visit and was trying to talk to her and she would have to call them back. Like all such encounters between true Southerners, this simple conversation took about twenty minutes.

But as I sat there contemplating how there were no right words for this conversation, I looked down at the table, and right before me, faceup and facing me, was a button with my grandmother's photo on it. I picked it up, looked closer, turned it over in my hand. I'd never seen this object in all of my life, but I knew immediately what it meant. A message that lay in that tired, small photo button of my grandmother's. It was an ID from the time she worked at the mill in Columbus. She looked skinny, worn down. A flat line where a smile should be. The back of the button was solid rust, as if it had spent the last fifty years buried in the dirt of a hundred thousand rains. The front side of the button with the photo was untouched.

In that moment I knew the message: I have been here and I have been where you are and I have survived. So will you. As painful as these days are, there are better days ahead. Go on, now, and do what you must do. Be strong. This is not the end of things but a new beginning.

My family didn't have that many things. I had grown up at my grandmother's side, played in her bedroom, sat at her little dresser, rummaged through the drawers. I'd never laid eyes on this thing, but I recognized her photo immediately. I held it, then passed it to my mother.

She cradles the button in her palm, slowly turns it over, examines the back, looks back at the photo.

"That's my mother!"

"I know."

"Where did you get this?"

"From your table right here." I point to the space in front of me.

"That's when she worked in the mill in Columbus." She looks at the button more closely. "She was only thirty-something there. And see how old she looks. I wasn't even born."

"Where'd it come from?" I asked this, but I had a feeling that I already knew.

"I don't know. I've never seen this before in my life."

Reading these pages outside of that moment, it may be difficult for you to understand the fact that this was a supernatural phenomenon. This identification button from circa 1920s surfaced at the exact moment I needed the courage to move forward in my life. It said everything I needed to hear without saying anything at all.

My sister soon arrived. She knew the news I was about to share with Mom. She was there for emotional support. I showed her the button.

"Where did you get that?" she asked me. "I've never seen this. And I have all of Grannie's old things: her purse, her jewelry, her handkerchiefs. I've never laid eyes on this."

"I know. Neither has Mom."

Neither had any other family member we showed it to. Because at that point, the button was getting pinned to my blue jean jacket and traveling with me for a thousand miles as I put some distance between me and a long decision. At night I would lie in a strange bed and unclip the button and hold in in my palm. Reach my hand up, as if I were catching something from a woman who loved me a long time ago. Who apparently still did.

As much as I might try to, I don't comprehend the theory of physics, matter, energy, and possibility. But I understand love. This thing happened. The love of God or the love of my grandmother or the love of both of them reached out to me on one of the darkest nights of my life and in the midst of a grave decision, and sent me a tangible sign. Whether it was that thing that Grandmother tossed me years ago in my dream, I don't know. What I cling to now is the knowledge alone that it happened. I wonder how, in the years that pass after my death, I would reach out and touch a loved one. What would I send that said, "Be strong and full of courage, for God is with you"? Perhaps this book is exactly that. It's my way of reaching out, saying, "Here are my stories, the things I've seen, heard, experienced. I am not different from you. I love *Guardians of the Galaxy* and the novel *Bel Canto*, fried chicken, and goat cheese. Red wine and good times."

I've wanted to search for a door, find the thin place where I can enter into the Heavenly Kingdom of God in this life. Now I realize I have. What I yearn to say to those long after I'm dead and gone, I'd like people to read my words and realize that the eternal mystery is right here. In the middle of our movies, our arguments, our sitting down to break bread at the table at home or out at Chili's. That mystery as we have a beer with a friend or hot tea with a sister. It's in our everyday communion in the smallest ways. Our hello to the desk clerk, our smile at a cashier. It's in every good deed, small kindness, and conversation.

Someday I may travel to all the thin places that my curiosity can afford. The holy places and meccas of my dreams. Where time has etched a hand that says here people sought and found. I will stand looking out on the world from the heights of Machu Picchu or wait to cross as the water recedes at the Isle of Iona. I'll travel to Ireland to look upon *The Book of Kells*, contemplating the hands that held those brushes to create. But I realize now it will not be a set of magical coordinates that opens the doorway. I've had what I've been searching for all along. It is within me. I am the thin place.

Acknowledgments

A very special thank-you to my mother, who has lived with me through the final edits of *Confessions* and offered herself as a patient sounding board during the process. To all of my family: sister Sheila, sons Nick and Chris, cousin Deb, and to the Adorables and the Charmings. You light my heart.

A special thank-you to Wendy Grisham, who brought me to the party. Long may your freak flag fly!

To my editor, Adrienne Ingrum, for your unfailing patience, great passion, and vision for the power of this story, I offer my utmost respect and gratitude. To Grace Johnson, for always being there, day or night, weekends, and break of day—you rock! And to all the FaithWords tribe: Every single one of you make up the whole that has brought this book into being. I am deeply thankful for your work.

Greg Daniel, it's been a lifetime in the making, and here it is. Thank you for talking me off more ledges now than I can count.

To my friend Carol Proctor, thank you for being God's graceful angel who steadies me when I grow weary and reminds me of the eternal vision.

To Dick Staub and Nigel Goodwin for founding the Kindlings

movement and bringing me into your fold with the greatest bonding story of all time. Which led me to lunch with Bobette Buster, a movie producer who wanted to discuss my upcoming projects. When I said, "I really want to write a book called *Confessions of a Christian Mystic*," she said, "Write that book! That is the book I want to buy. That is the book I want to read." So, gentlemen, this book exists because of you.

To the wild women of the Nashville Dutch Lunch Bunch: I don't want to even think where I would be or what life would be like without your love and support, laughter and understanding. You amaze me one and all!

To my Clearstory Radio friends and family of Radio Free Nashville, WRFN 107.1 Nashville: Your support on air and off means the world to me.

To the writing students from the Phonebooth Writer Series, thank you for always reminding me to write wild, practice what I preach, and to not pull my punches.

A very special shout-out to my Undercover Reader Posse. You have been right there with me all along the way. Thank you for your early reads and for being part of my story.

And to all my readers, thank you for letting me be a part of your unfolding story as you read *Confessions*.

Peace to all everywhere.

About the Author

River Jordan is an author, speaker, teacher, and radio host. She has written four novels, and her nonfiction book is *Praying for Strangers: An Adventure of the Human Spirit*. She travels the country speaking on *The Power of Story*, is a regular contributor to *Psychology Today's Spirituality* blog, and is the host and producer of the literary radio program *Clearstory Radio*, which airs from Nashville, where she makes her home.

Reading Group Guide

1. INTO THE MYSTIC
What is the story of your birth? Was it one that was experienced with joy? Or was it more like the author's and bittersweet? Our lives have many types of birth stories, many new beginnings: marriage, the birth of a child, a move, a new job. What are the favorite birth stories in your life? What new birth stories would you like to see unfold in your life?

2. THE DREAM READERS
River's life shows that others influence our way of being and believing from a very young age. How have your childhood influences shaped who you are today? How do the people now in your life—associations, groups, and social media—continue to have an effect on the person you are?

3. THE COMPREHENSION OF THEOLOGICAL REALITIES
What historical happenings have been markers in your life? Identify those that have been a force leading to a positive outcome and those that instilled fear. Have you been able to hold on to your beliefs or your faith even when what happened was not what you wanted?

4. IN PRIMITIVE SPACE

The author describes a faith-filled congregation whose memory brought her great comfort. Then, years later, that same group of people deeply hurt someone she loved. Did this harm erase the good? How do you handle your disappointment in others?

5. POCKETBOOK SAINTS

River's experience shows that our heroes come in all shapes and sizes. And they come with oddities we might not expect. In a day when our culture is so prolific at promoting cookie-cutter heroes and heroines, challenge yourself to discover heroic qualities in everyday people.

Do you find it is more difficult to see yourself as someone else's hero or to imagine that you might be the hero of your own story? Given the opportunity to stand up and speak up for someone else, would you do so? If not, why not? How could you make a course correction to advocate for the weak or unprotected?

6. MEMENTO MORI

How did you first learn of the reality of death? Which best describes how you approach this subject now: Do you push it from your mind and just don't think about it? Or do you have everything listed, planned, and decided in advance? What could you do that would bring you more peace about death? How might you gently bring that peace to others?

7. SALVATION IN THE SEA OATS

The author finds a spiritual home in the Episcopal church and a role model in the retired priest of her story. What place has felt like your spiritual home? What friends, teachers, or pastors have been an example to you along the way? How do these influences continue to touch and affect your life today?

8. A SHOT OF JESUS AND A SNIPPET OF TRUTH

The author communicates by letter with a friend to discuss faith. Write a letter to a friend with whom you'd like to discuss your faith—without judging theirs.

9. MARK TWAIN HAS A TWITCH

The author enjoys the work of authors like Mark Twain because their stories enable her to discern their passions and what is important to them. What storytellers—authors, movie-makers, songwriters—hold power for you? What storytelling messages ring true with you?

10. THE TIMELY ART OF INSPIRATION

Some people believe in messengers and some don't. For those who feel the right word in due season is like rain in a desert drought, messengers can be meaningful. When did you find a specific direction in your life for which you were seeking? Did it alter your decisions and change your path? Or did the messenger simply confirm what your heart or gut was saying and give you the courage to continue?

11. THE LAST DANCE

There are many seasons in life, and not all of them feel full of light. Sometimes a season can feel dark. Have you sustained dark days when the light of life seldom broke through? What has helped the light to break through for you? Where were you able to find relief, peace, and comfort?

12. MAD DOG JACK
The midnight hour is when friends often share their secrets. Have you ever shared a secret that you were afraid to share for fear of being outcast, shamed, or ridiculed? Has a friend ever shared a secret with you that surprised you? How did you handle this sharing of uncomfortable secrets?

13. EMMET TELLS A STORY
Sometimes we are most surprised by the kindness of a stranger, the gentleness of the strong, and the deep strength of the meek. Those who have had encounters with the Divine can be surprised by both the simplicity and magnitude of the experience. Have you ever been caught by surprise or left speechless in such an encounter?

14. WHEN FIRST WE LEARN OF NO TOMORROWS
River instructs a granddaughter to live out her life with "a courageous and fearless passion." What words would you offer today to someone who might discover them after you're gone? What do you consider to be the single most important truth of your life that you could share with others?

15. SIGNS AND WONDERS IN ORDINARY TIME
The author fears the thing she desires the most, but eventually she can laugh at her fears in the process of admitting them and ultimately receive a gift that eclipses her expectations. What is it you most desire to see? Is it also something you fear?

16. A SLOE GIN FIZZ AND THE MYERS-BRIGGS
What personality tests have you taken? Did you find the results confirming or revealing? Did the results help you better

understand yourself or relate better to others? Could finding your "type" become just a trap for labeling both yourself and others?

17. ON RUMI AND THE TONGUES OF ANGELS
In relating "the language of angels," the author reveals a secret side of herself. Do you keep certain cards close to the vest for fear of the opinions of others? Does this position strengthen or weaken you?

18. THE HAPPENSTANCE OF GHOSTS AND OTHER MATTER
Discuss occurrences in your life that have piqued your interest in the marriage of science and faith.

19. KUNG FU COMMUNION
There's an old joke about a dog chasing a car, never knowing what he would do if he actually caught it. When people chase after God, they chase after a Creator who might surprise them. Do you consider yourself a God chaser? What do you expect to find?

20. ON MYSTICS AND SEXUAL HEALING
In one late-night conversation with other women around a table, the author is suddenly presented with a question that distills down to one line what she believes. What would that question be for you?

21. FULL MOONS CAST THE LONGEST SHADOWS
Revisit a moment of such peace that you seemed to lose your mind and find your soul.

22. MERGE WITH CAUTION

The author admits to experiences both strange and wondrous, but she cautions us to not live by supernatural moments and rely instead on the more human ones, which perhaps tax our nerves and require patience. Recall an ordinary beauty in your life that you saw as breathtaking in scope. What would it take for you to see every day this way?

23. THE GOD PICTURE

Draw something: The best day you've ever had. The best part of a relationship. The most love you've ever felt. The moment you first looked up and beheld the stars. Some things cannot be captured in their full scope—not in images, in words, or in song. But the magnificence is in trying.

24. THE VEIL OF THE VATICAN

The author is surprised by what she experiences in a visit to the Vatican. Describe a physical place that surprised you with its sense of history, power, and presence.

25. WALKABOUTS AND RIPTIDES

The author shares the story that a friend describes in his book *The Singing Bowl* about his journey of faith and what some would call Divine timing: Despite not carrying a map, he was in exactly the right place at exactly the right time. Recall a moment in life where your path seemed to be aligned with the stars, as if the entire universe had conspired to get you to that place at that time. Do you feel that same guiding hand is operating and directing what might be perceived as the more mundane details of your daily life? Could you look at everyday moments as a little more spectacular?

26. MESSENGERS AND MERCURY

Scriptures reference the cloud of witnesses who look down upon us. If you were to assemble a cloud of witnesses to cheer you on—be they people from your own life, from history, or fictitious characters—who would they be and why?

27–31. NAKED CAME I

How do you view nudity: as acceptable or non-acceptable? How important is it that our hearts remain unclothed and naked before God and each other?

32. DOG AND CAT TAKE A RIDE

The author recounts a road trip and book tour with a fellow author and believer. They have a lot of similarities but also striking differences. How have friendships with people different from yourself helped you grow as a person or accept the differences of others? In a time of increasing tribalism, schisms, and divisions, can friendships with those of different opinions serve as a bridge to better communication?

33. THE ZOMBIE TRUTH

The end of time can wear many faces. It can be the end of a marriage, the death of a loved one, the end of a career, or a natural disaster. The events that trigger the end-of-days mentality require us to show what we are truly made of. How will we choose to survive, and will we help others to do the same? What events in your life have shown you your true mettle? In what ways have you surprised yourself or disappointed yourself? How can you prepare mentally, physically, and spiritually for the end times?

34. LUCY BOARDS A TRAIN

In what moments were you able to transcend the noise of your life to be fully alive? What was the catalyst that helped you get there?

35. THE WHISTLE CALLS MY NAME

The author imagines a death experience and compares it to boarding a train for a final destination. The focus of the story is on letting go of the physical life and stepping into the unseen spiritual life. Describe what you perceive the crossing into an afterlife to be like. Does your description bring you comfort or sorrow? What would you hope for yourself and your loved ones to discover at this inevitable moment?

36. A GYPSY DAUGHTER'S DISSIPATION

The author describes an experience as a child that called to her soul, whispered to her of another life that was very different from hers and the traditions of her people. Have you ever felt called to something that was "other" and very much beyond the borders of your familiar experiences? Describe what happened when you answered that call. Or explore why you were afraid to do so.

37. AN ENCOUNTER OF MYSTICAL PROPORTIONS

Have you encountered natural creatures along your journey that have left strong impressions with you? Did you sense a slice of the Divine that left you reverential?

38. HANGING OUT IN THE LATE-NIGHT HACIENDA

Quiet sometimes finds us and takes us by surprise. Other times we must fight to create a place for retreat—or we simply book one, despite worldly circumstances that conspire against us.

Recall times in your life when quiet found you: perhaps an unexpected day off, the first snow of the season, a vacation. Were you able to hear that still small voice and rebalance your priorities?

39–41. TO CUSS OR NOT TO CUSS, CHRISTIAN TRIBES, A COAT OF MANY COLORS

In these chapters the author reflects on many of the subjects that seem to be affecting her faith and defining Christian subgroups that all feel their brand of Christianity is "the right one." How does your faith allow room for those with different opinions? How does Jesus and the scriptural example of his life join groups together to provide common ground?

42. THE DEATH OF DESIRE

Often heartbreak sows seeds of hidden anger and springs thorns of unforgiveness. The garden of the heart, though cleaned and cleared just last week, has found new memories that reap new pain, like weeds that must be checked daily. How do you visit forgiveness? In what ways do you find the strength to hold on to forgiveness as a perpetual shield? How can you help others do the same without appearing self-righteous?

43. PORN AND POPCORN

The proliferation of pornography through the internet has touched countless lives. Is it possible to have a conversation about what a healthy sex life entails without it turning to judgment and condemnation?

44. WHERE WE BEGIN AGAIN

What are three things you wish you could "wipe clean" in your life? What would a "brand-new day" mean to you?

45. THE BOONDOCK BLESSING

Stories on the big screen are large, powerful, influential, and entertaining. What movies speak to you and have withstood the test of time because they tell a portion of your story? What movies have become a part of your family holiday traditions? As you stand back and consider them, what do they say to you about who you are and your life?

46. BODY SURFING THE ASTRAL PLANE

Name one thing that happened to you that is truly beyond any earthly or logical explanation.

47. THE COMPANY WE KEEP

Consider the company you keep, through social media, the literature you read, and the movies and TV shows you watch. What are you feeding yourself? If you succumbed to the influences and emulated those around you, what would you begin to look like and sound like? Is that the real you, the one you want to be and project to the world?

48. WE ARE LOST IN TRANSLATION

How do you believe your faith may write a new story? Envision that your "side" doesn't win and you come to a place of quiet understanding within yourself. What images would be part of that vision?

49. A LABYRINTH IN THE TWILIGHT

The author walks a labyrinth for the first time, and though she is very distracted and far from a "spiritual state of mind," it turns out to be a richly rewarding and profoundly impactful experience. What experiences help you find your way to the "heart of God"?

50. A SIMPLE MOLECULAR MANIFESTATION

The author shares a gift from her grandmother that found its way to her when she needed it most and conveyed a much-needed message for courage and continuing: "Be strong and be of good courage, for I am with you and God is with you—always." If you needed to send such a message to a loved one long after you were gone, what form would it take? (Would it be a letter, art, needlework, a fine piece of carpentry?) How can you share those sentiments with your friends and family right now?